AMERICAN POETS PROJECT

The American Poets Project is published

with a gift in memory of
JAMES MERRILL

and support from the
SIDNEY J. WEINBERG, JR. FOUNDATION

Edgar
Allan Poe

poems and poetics

richard wilbur editor

AMERICAN POETS PROJECT

THE LIBRARY OF AMERICA

Design by Chip Kidd and Mark Melnick.

Library of Congress Cataloging-in-Publication Data:
Poe, Edgar Allan, 1809–1849.
[Selections. 2003]
Poems and poetics / Edgar Allan Poe ; Richard Wilbur, editor.
    p. cm. — (American poets project)
Includes bibliographical references and index.
ISBN 1–931082–51–0 (alk. paper)
    I. Wilbur, Richard. II. Title. III. Series
PS2605.A1 2003
811'3 — dc21
2003046637
10 9 8 7 6 5 4 3 2 1

Edgar
Allan
Poe

CONTENTS

INTRODUCTION

Aldous Huxley held that "all the poems of Poe are spells," and that "The City in the Sea" was his best spell of all. That Poe himself thought of poetry in terms of spell-casting is made plain in his criticism, where he praises Tennyson for employing "a suggestive indefinitiveness of meaning, with the view of bringing about a definitiveness of vague and therefore of spiritual *effect*." A spell or charm deals in "*effect*," not meaningful content, and in fact it was anciently believed that if a charm went so far as to include the name of its subject, it would not work. Poe's spellbinding is not so absolute as that, but the content or meaning of his poems is often muffled by the incantation, repetition, sonority, and hypnotic rhythm of his technique, especially in the later work. His richest writing is to be found in the finest of his tales; yet, despite its extreme exclusions and self-limitations, the poetry has its memorable triumphs ("Ulalume" and "Annabel Lee," for instance) in the vein of sorcery. Actually, this writer thinks that Poe's most powerful spell is to be found in the relatively clear final stanza of "To One in Paradise":

> And all my days are trances,
> And all my nightly dreams
> Are where thy grey eye glances,
> And where thy footstep gleams—
> In what ethereal dances,
> By what eternal streams.

Something that contributed to Poe's use of incantatory and mesmeric techniques was the popularity, in his day, of recitation. Poems such as "The Raven" and "The Bells," with their compelling rhythms and their dramatic changes of tone, were suitable for parlor or stage performance—and were for many years declaimed in the schoolrooms of America. The Poe scholar T. O. Mabbott tells us that "Ulalume" was commissioned, for purposes of recitation, by Colesworth P. Bronson, an Episcopal minister and a celebrated elocutionist. Poe himself was a fine platform performer. In October 1845 he was invited to read a poem at the Boston Lyceum where, unable to write a new poem for the occasion, he first offered "Al Aaraaf" and then—by request—"The Raven." Years later Thomas Wentworth Higginson remembered the delivery of "Al Aaraaf" this way:

> The verses had long since been printed in his youthful volume . . . and they produced no very distinct impression on the audience till Poe began to read the maiden's song in the second part. Already his tones had been softening to a finer melody than at first, and when he came to the verses,—
>
> > Ligeia! Ligeia!
> > My beautiful one!

his voice seemed attenuated to the faintest golden thread; the audience became hushed, and, as it were, breathless; there seemed no life in the hall but his; and every syllable was accentuated with such delicacy, and sustained with such sweetness, as I never heard equaled by other lips. When the lyric ended, it was like the ceasing of the gypsy's chant in Browning's "Flight of the Duchess"; and I remember nothing more, except that in walking back to Cambridge my comrades and I felt that we had been under the spell of some wizard. Indeed, I feel much the same in the retrospect, to this day.

There is, of course, more than mumbo-jumbo to be found in Poe's verse, especially in the earlier work, and in showing this I will have to dwell a bit on the content of "Al Aaraaf," that youthful poem (little read today) in which Higginson discovered such incantatory power.

In a letter of 1829, addressed to the publisher Isaac Lea and enclosing a manuscript of verse, the young Edgar Allan Poe declared himself "irrecoverably a poet," and included these jaunty lines to the same effect:

> It was my choice or chance or curse
> To adopt the cause for better or worse
> And with my worldly goods and wit
> And soul and body worship it.

However much Poe felt himself wedded to poetry, the familiar facts of his life readily explain why his body of work in that medium is so small. Finding himself cut off in his early twenties by his guardian John Allan, and so without hope of aid or inheritance, he made his way into magazine work, and for the rest of his life—in Richmond, Philadelphia, or New York—was a hard-working editor, fiction writer, and critic for various publications. He worked both hard and well, was very poor, and on rare occasions resorted to drink, which his system could not tolerate. What steadied him was that he lived with and supported his aunt Maria Clemm and her daughter Virginia, who at thirteen became his "child-bride," and whose death in 1847 began the disintegration of his final years. Poe's was not a life in which much energy could be allotted for the writing of unprofitable poems, and it was not until the celebrity of "The Raven" that any verse of his had notable success. In his brief preface to *The Raven and Other Poems* (1845), Poe described its contents as "trifles," and ruefully wrote, "Events not to be controlled have prevented me from making, at any time, any serious effort in what, under happier circumstances, would have been the field of my choice."

The title poem of *Tamerlane and Other Poems*, Poe's first book, was in final form a Byronic monologue of 243 lines, and "Al Aaraaf," the longest poem in his second book (*Al Aaraaf, Tamerlane and Minor Poems*), was a two-part cosmic vision 422 lines long. Poe began, in other words, with a capacity for sustained performance in verse, and in the case of "Al Aaraaf" for fullness of argument. Despite its involutions and elaborations, which have bogged down many a reader, the latter poem is an intelligible statement of what Poe the critic would be saying twenty years later, in "The Poetic Principle," regarding the nature of poetry ("a wild effort to reach the Beauty above") and its relation to the faculties of "Pure Intellect, Taste, and the Moral Sense."

Part I of "Al Aaraaf" presents us with a wandering star of that name, which Poe identifies both with a kind of dreamers' limbo out of Mohammedan mythology and with a short-lived nova, discovered by Tycho Brahe in

1572, which was briefly framed by four stars in the constellation of Cassiopeia. The star Al Aaraaf is ruled by Nesace, the spirit of Beauty, and though it is barred from the vicinity of Heaven, whose seraphs enjoy an intellectual knowledge of divine things, it has an important cosmic function. Its assignment is to mediate between Heaven and the far-flung spheres of the creation, inducing in them a purely aesthetic sense of universal order, and chastening them if they presume to a species of knowledge for which they are not yet eligible. It appears that Al Aaraaf has in a recent century paid a visit to our Earth, seeking to purify it lest its intellectual presumption be contagious, and "the stars totter in the guilt of man." It is also implied that if the scattered cosmos—the stars and their occupants—will cleave to an aesthetic apprehension of things, all will ultimately be called home and regathered in God. Al Aaraaf is the marshal of that movement.

Bathed in clouds that filter out all but the beauty of the universe, Al Aaraaf is peopled by angels and poetic souls, some of them recruited from such worlds as ours, for whom the chief activity is to dream. The flowers of Al Aaraaf, to which the poem gives much attention, are in some cases the prototypes of those that grow elsewhere, while others have been transplanted from the gardens of Earth and other stars. In further respects, too, Al Aaraaf is both the disseminator and the conservator of beauty: the palace of Nesace incorporates "Friezes from Tadmor and Persepolis," "Achaian statues," and other exquisite trophies from the Earth's youth—from a time when our planet had not yet been corrupted by scientific thought and, what Poe would call in *Eureka*, "the conventional World-Reason."

"Al Aaraaf" is chiefly concerned with the laying-out of a cosmic vision, and the poem's element of narrative can be briefly summarized. In Part I, Nesace kneels and addresses a dutiful silent prayer to God, who responds by commanding her to resume her corrective embassy to the spheres of his creation. In Part II, Nesace sings a song that, addressing itself especially to Ligeia, the spirit of Harmony, urges the denizens of her star to awaken from their dreams and do God's will. The only other event is that two of her subjects, Angelo and Ianthe, fail to answer Nesace's summons because they "hear not for the beating of their hearts." The point of this closing episode is that passion, for subordinate spirits and lesser angels, is not compatible with the highest aesthetic purposes.

Poe's well-turned and well-known "Sonnet—To Science" was often printed as an introduction to "Al Aaraaf," and it is possible, taking the two poems in sequence, to derive from them the story of a poet's career. This poet, born on our planet at a time when science and "harsh mathematical reason" (Poe's phrase from "The Colloquy of Monos and Una") were gaining the ascendant, is yet able in his younger years to see the world with a visionary eye; resisting the zeitgeist and his own temptation to comply with it, he sees Diana in the moon, jewels in the skies, naiads in every stream. In time, however, the prosaic, utilitarian spirit of the age so afflicts him, and so corrupts the aspect of his earthly environment, that his dreaming imagination must "seek a shelter in some happier star," forsaking mundane "truth" for such supernal beauty as can be found in Al Aaraaf, and replacing his lost naiads with the angelic likes of Nesace and Ligeia. In turning both inward and away from Earth, Poe's poet is a spirit oppressed and in flight; yet as he will subsequently make clear in the prose piece "The Power of Words," his poet's dreams not only find shelter in beautiful stars but can imagine them into being; furthermore, as in the prose-poem *Eureka*

(1848), the poet's dreams of harmony will powerfully contribute to the reattunement of the diffused cosmos and its final reunion in and as God. Poe's poet is, in short, both a victim and a potential deity.

The plot of "Sonnet—To Science" and "Al Aaraaf," if the two early poems are taken together, amounts to the fullest and most significant narrative in Poe's verse *oeuvre*. Thereafter, Poe's myth of poetic soul, ever his fundamental story, was best told in his prose tales, where his treatment of it can be wonderfully artful, varied, and subtle. The prose tale, as Poe said in his criticism, is a form in which Truth—concreteness, clarity, logic, detail—occupies the surface; but in truly imaginative fiction, he adds, there will always be "beneath the transparent upper current of meaning an under or *suggestive* one." A suggestible reader will find a number of tales ("MS. Found in a Bottle," "The Domain of Arnheim") that describe in the form of an inward journey a soul's recovery of its first spiritual condition—tales that proceed by way of growing solitude, somnolence, and hypnagogic visions toward a dreamy plunge into the transcendent. There are also tales of psychic conflict, as diverse in flavor as "The Duc De l'Omelette," "William Wilson," and "The Purloined Letter," in which the hero defends the purity of a Nesace-figure against his corrupt and worldly double. In "The Fall of the House of Usher" the union of Roderick and Madeline in death depicts the purification and reintegration of a soul, while the crumbling of their mansion prefigures the collapse of the material cosmos into its primal unity. As for that great story "Ligeia," it retells in its way the basic plot that we have just extracted from "Sonnet—To Science" and "Al Aaraaf." The heroine, as many insistent suggestions convey, is allegorically an angelic spirit like her namesake in "Al Aaraaf." Under her influence the hero (who on the story's *suggestive* level is a child) communes with God by way of the harmony and beauty of the arts and of nature. When Ligeia is lost to him, the hero is "but as a child groping benighted." In time he lovelessly marries an earthly woman named Rowena, and establishes her in a bridal chamber that represents his own bereaved and dreaming mind: wildly eclectic furnishings express its freedom from space and time, the perpetual agitation of figured draperies evokes the hypnagogic state, and a gold-chained censer hangs from the center of the ceiling, emitting "parti-colored fires" and recalling that gold-chained diamond window atop Nesace's palace, which diffracts the rays of God's truth into the colors of Beauty. In such a milieu, the earthly Rowena sickens, wastes away, and is at last transmuted into the restored Ligeia, who beneath the central censer opens her profound eyes and looses her raven hair. In Wordsworthian terms, the poet-hero has—briefly, at least—got back "the glory and the dream" of his prophetic childhood.

In his tales Poe is surely the most difficult of the symbolic writers of his century, yet with patience we may sound his submerged meanings, finding in the best of his stories a complete narrative and a self-sufficient statement of his essential themes. Completeness of plot and idea, however, are rarer in Poe's verse after the long poems of his youth, and his lectures and criticism were to develop a theory of poetry in which such completeness is inessential. "The Valley of Unrest" is a characteristic poem that, in itself, gives an extremely attenuated account of how a nameless "people" have left their happy valley and "gone unto the wars," leaving behind a "nameless grave," a stagnant atmosphere, and self-agitated trees and flowers that shake for grief and weep "Eternal dews." The reader, in his anxiety for a fuller narrative, might turn to the later prose tale "Eleonora," with its changeable valley and its Ligeia-like heroine who dies and is buried among "eye-like violets that writhed uneasily and were ever encumbered with dew." Undoubtedly the poem influenced the writing of "Eleonora"; with slight adjustments it could be seen within the frame of that classic story and thus "explained." Yet the poem itself seems satisfied to create, as it does, an uncanny landscape in which clouds and flora are moved, in a physical sense, by sorrow and remorse.

"The Haunted Palace," in which another valley changes for the worse, is a more intelligible story-poem whose central conceit or enigma is finely articulated. The palace of the title, as the reader soon divines, is the head of a man who has golden hair, bright eyes, rosy lips, and pearly teeth. Within the head is harmonious thought and from the man's mouth come continual "wit and wisdom." In the final stanzas, however, the "monarch Thought" is deposed by "evil things, in robes of sorrow," and his palace becomes, as Poe told Rufus Griswold in a letter of 1841, "a mind haunted by phantoms—a disordered brain." The man's final condition—his bloodshot eyes, his jangled reason, his mad laughter—is clearly symbolized, but the stated cause of his mental decline—those "evil things"—is extremely vague. The poem is interested in making a brilliant before-and-after depiction of a mind, but not in the thorough spinning of a tale.

There are certain of Poe's later poems that unfold in argument quite plainly. The sonnet "To My Mother," addressed to his mother-in-law (and aunt) Maria Clemm, develops its thought with a leisured grace within the divisions of the form. A less regular sonnet, called "Sonnet—Silence," discourses logically upon two kinds of death, the death of the body and the death of the soul. But in Poe, thinking, like narration, is customarily somewhat crumpled or obscured. For this writer, it took decades of acquaintance with "Israfel" before it become apparent that the poem is an implicit essay on the facultative basis of poetry on Earth and in Heaven. The earthly poet of the poem's last stanza is restricted to singing a "mortal melody." That is, in accordance with Poe's poetics (as stated in "The Poetic Principle") he must seek to glimpse supernal Beauty through the aesthetic sense alone, which "unless incidentally . . . has no concern whatever with Duty or with Truth" and which has nothing to do with the heart and its passions. For the angel Israfel, whose "heart-strings are a lute," it is otherwise:

> . . . the skies that angel trod,
>   Where deep thoughts are a duty—
>   Where Love's a grown-up God—
>   Where the Houri glances are
>   Imbued with all the beauty
>   Which we worship in a star.

If one extricates the thought from the strong musicality and deceptive near-banality of those lines, it is clear that Israfel's song can bring into concert all the elements of his nature—the sense of beauty, the intellect ("deep thoughts"), the moral sense ("duty"), and the passionate heart in a way not possible for man in what Poe calls (in "The Colloquy of Monos and Una") "the infant condition of his soul."

We are to admire the inclusive angelic consciousness that our grown-up souls may someday achieve. But meanwhile our poetry, in Poe's view, must specialize in aesthetic transcendence, eschewing the truth, morality, and passion that might entangle it with this present world. The whole movement of Poe's poetry is away from the material here and now. "To Helen" and "The Coliseum" yearn back toward Earth's glorious youth; other poems escape into visions, into dreamland, into what Poe calls in "The Sleeper" the "conscious slumber" of the dead; the fine late poem "Eldorado" says that only beyond the grave will desire be answered. Two lines from an early draft of "The Valley of Unrest" say simply: "All things lovely—are not they / Far away—far away?" And the charming poem "Evening Star" embodies that formula, rejecting the Earth's "lowly" moon in favor of Venus' "distant" and celestial beauty.

The reader of "Evening Star" will notice that the *enshrouding* of the moon by a cloud increases the visibility of Venus, just as the death and enshrouding of Rowena makes possible a vision of Ligeia. Poe could sometimes seem to say, as in his review of Thomas Moore's *Alciphron*, that imaginative verse approaches unearthly beauty by way of earthly loveliness: "In every glimpse of beauty presented, we catch, through long and wild vistas, dim bewildering visions of a far more ethereal beauty *beyond*." But it would be more exact to say, in Poe's case, that the poet's strategy is to accomplish a mock-destruction of earthly things, estranging the reader from material reality and so, presumably, propelling his imagination toward the ideal. Poe employs various magical means toward that end: vagueness of plot or argument, the sort of paradox ("Bottomless vales" from "Dream-Land") that renders an object inconceivable, a stress not on emotion—which might detain us on Earth—but on the *frisson* or "tremulous delight" (from "The Lake—To—") that might attend the imaginary destruction of our familiar environment. The poems are full of properties that distance us from the sensible world—silence, dimness, shadowiness, the fog that wraps the ruin of "The Sleeper," that mist that hangs upon the trees in "Spirits of the Dead." And everywhere, of course, there is the theme of dissolution and death. Some scholars have made the mistake of seeing necrophilia in all the moldering that goes on in Poe, and there are a few gruesome lines like "Soft may the worms about her creep!" (from "The Sleeper") that might support the charge of morbidity. But something quite different is intended. The hero of "Ligeia" begins in a "dim and decaying city by the Rhine," and ends in an English abbey with "verdant decay hanging about it." The point of all the crumbling, tottering architecture in Poe's fiction is that it is inhabited by visionaries who are subjectively dematerializing the realm of solid fact in quest of a bodiless beauty. (The dead ladies of the poems and tales also represent, among other things, "beauty heightened in dissolution," as Poe wrote in a review of poems by Joseph Rodman Drake and Fitz-Greene Halleck.) However we may interpret that famous poem "The City in the Sea," which draws upon Gomorrah's past and future fates and some apocalyptic passages from the Bible, it plainly imagines a vast descent of matter into the Nothing which was for Poe the threshold of the spiritual.

This volume includes a number of slighter pieces that the reader will readily identify as such: poems of gratitude to Poe's benefactress Marie Louise Shew, bits of literary flirtation addressed to the poetess Frances S. Osgood, poems for young ladies' albums, sometimes involving clever acrostics. Though free with references to stars and angels, these compositions, like the little song "Eulalie," could not possibly be classed, for depth and art, with such a major poem as "For Annie." The volume also includes a selection of relevant prose, including Poe's prefaces to his books of verse and a number of texts and excerpts that in one way or another illuminate the poems. A passage from "The Poetic Principle" and another from a review of R. H. Horne's *Orion* outline Poe's conception of poetry's concerns and scope, while other selections give his view of the imagination, telling how this supreme faculty differs from fancy, how it favors the indefinite and resembles visionary dream, and how by a "chemistry of the intellect" it can destructively transcend the elements with which it works. In "The Power of Words" and the conclusion of *Eureka: A Prose Poem* Poe addresses the relations of the cosmos and the creative soul.

The most unusual poem in this book—"Fairy-Land"—is by no means minor, though sometimes accounted so. It deals in the moons and mists of Poe's normal dream-scenery, but does so with a fluent inventiveness, and interrupts its imaginative flow with self-mocking collapses into the prosaic. It is hard to say why this apparently conflicted poem should work so well—why its prosaic collapses should somehow enhance the lyric verve of the lines, and why the poem as a whole should affect us as poignant and moving. It was Elizabeth Bishop's favorite Poe poem, and it is one of my favorites too. It is, perhaps, magical.

Richard Wilbur
2003

POEMS

Tamerlane

Kind solace in a dying hour!
    Such, father, is not (now) my theme—
I will not madly deem that power
        Of Earth may shrive me of the sin
        Unearthly pride hath revell'd in—
    I have no time to dote or dream:
You call it hope—that fire of fire!
It is but agony of desire:
If I *can* hope—Oh God! I can—
    Its fount is holier—more divine—
I would not call thee fool, old man,
    But such is not a gift of thine.

Know thou the secret of a spirit
    Bow'd from its wild pride into shame.
O yearning heart! I did inherit
    Thy withering portion with the fame,
The searing glory which hath shone
Amid the Jewels of my throne,
Halo of Hell! and with a pain
Not Hell shall make me fear again—
O craving heart, for the lost flowers
And sunshine of my summer hours!
The undying voice of that dead time,
With its interminable chime,
Rings, in the spirit of a spell,
Upon thy emptiness—a knell.

I have not always been as now:
The fever'd diadem on my brow
    I claim'd and won usurpingly—
Hath not the same fierce heirdom given
    Rome to the Cæsar—this to me?
        The heritage of a kingly mind,
And a proud spirit which hath striven
        Triumphantly with human kind.

On mountain soil I first drew life:
    The mists of the Taglay have shed
    Nightly their dews upon my head,
And, I believe, the winged strife
And tumult of the headlong air
Have nestled in my very hair.

So late from Heaven—that dew—it fell
    ('Mid dreams of an unholy night)
Upon me with the touch of Hell,
    While the red flashing of the light
From clouds that hung, like banners, o'er,
    Appeared to my half-closing eye
    The pageantry of monarchy,
And the deep trumpet-thunder's roar
    Came hurriedly upon me, telling
        Of human battle, where my voice,
    My own voice, silly child!—was swelling
        (O! how my spirit would rejoice,
And leap within me at the cry)
The battle-cry of Victory!

The rain came down upon my head
    Unshelter'd—and the heavy wind
    Rendered me mad and deaf and blind.
It was but man, I thought, who shed
    Laurels upon me: and the rush—
The torrent of the chilly air
Gurgled within my ear the crush
    Of empires—with the captive's prayer—
The hum of suitors—and the tone
Of flattery 'round a sovereign's throne.

My passions, from that hapless hour,
    Usurp'd a tyranny which men
Have deem'd, since I have reach'd to power,
        My innate nature—be it so:
    But, father, there liv'd one who, then,
Then—in my boyhood—when their fire
        Burn'd with a still intenser glow
(For passion must, with youth, expire)
    E'en *then* who knew this iron heart
    In woman's weakness had a part.

I have no words—alas!—to tell
The loveliness of loving well!
Nor would I now attempt to trace
The more than beauty of a face
Whose lineaments, upon my mind,
Are——shadows on th' unstable wind:
Thus I remember having dwelt
    Some page of early lore upon,
With loitering eye, till I have felt

The letters—with their meaning—melt
　　To fantasies—with none.

O, she was worthy of all love!
　　Love—as in infancy was mine—
'Twas such as angel minds above
　　Might envy; her young heart the shrine
On which my every hope and thought
　　Were incense—then a goodly gift,
　　　For they were childish and upright—
Pure——as her young example taught:
　　Why did I leave it, and, adrift,
　　　Trust to the fire within, for light?

We grew in age—and love—together—
　　Roaming the forest, and the wild;
My breast her shield in wintry weather—
　　And, when the friendly sunshine smil'd,
And she would mark the opening skies,
I saw no Heaven—but in her eyes.

Young Love's first lesson is——the heart:
　　For 'mid that sunshine, and those smiles,
When, from our little cares apart,
　　And laughing at her girlish wiles,
I'd throw me on her throbbing breast,
　　And pour my spirit out in tears—
There was no need to speak the rest—
　　No need to quiet any fears
Of her—who ask'd no reason why,
But turn'd on me her quiet eye!

Yet *more* than worthy of the love
My spirit struggled with, and strove,
When, on the mountain peak, alone,
Ambition lent it a new tone—
I had no being—but in thee:
    The world, and all it did contain
In the earth—the air—the sea—
    Its joy—its little lot of pain
That was new pleasure——the ideal,
    Dim, vanities of dreams by night—
And dimmer nothings which were real—
    (Shadows—and a more shadowy light!)
Parted upon their misty wings,
        And, so, confusedly, became
        Thine image and—a name—a name!
Two separate—yet most intimate things.

I was ambitious—have you known
        The passion, father? You have not:
A cottager, I mark'd a throne
Of half the world as all my own,
        And murmur'd at such lowly lot—
But, just like any other dream,
        Upon the vapor of the dew
My own had past, did not the beam
        Of beauty which did while it thro'
The minute—the hour—the day—oppress
My mind with double loveliness.

We walk'd together on the crown
Of a high mountain which look'd down

Afar from its proud natural towers
  Of rock and forest, on the hills—
The dwindled hills! begirt with bowers
  And shouting with a thousand rills.

I spoke to her of power and pride,
  But mystically—in such guise
That she might deem it nought beside
  The moment's converse; in her eyes
I read, perhaps too carelessly—
  A mingled feeling with my own—
The flush on her bright cheek, to me
  Seem'd to become a queenly throne
Too well that I should let it be
  Light in the wilderness alone.

I wrapp'd myself in grandeur then
  And donn'd a visionary crown——
    Yet it was not that Fantasy
    Had thrown her mantle over me—
But that, among the rabble—men,
  Lion ambition is chain'd down—
And crouches to a keeper's hand—
Not so in deserts where the grand—
The wild—the terrible conspire
With their own breath to fan his fire.

Look 'round thee now on Samarcand!—
  Is she not queen of Earth? her pride
Above all cities? in her hand
  Their destinies? in all beside

Of glory which the world hath known
Stands she not nobly and alone?
Falling—her veriest stepping-stone
Shall form the pedestal of a throne—
And who her sovereign? Timour—he
   Whom the astonished people saw
Striding o'er empires haughtily
   A diadem'd outlaw!

O, human love! thou spirit given,
On Earth, of all we hope in Heaven!
Which fall'st into the soul like rain
Upon the Siroc-wither'd plain,
And, failing in thy power to bless,
But leav'st the heart a wilderness!
Idea! which bindest life around
With music of so strange a sound
And beauty of so wild a birth—
Farewell! for I have won the Earth.

When Hope, the eagle that tower'd, could see
   No cliff beyond him in the sky,
His pinions were bent droopingly—
   And homeward turn'd his soften'd eye.
'Twas sunset: when the sun will part
There comes a sullenness of heart
To him who still would look upon
The glory of the summer sun.
That soul will hate the ev'ning mist
So often lovely, and will list
To the sound of the coming darkness (known

To those whose spirits harken) as one
Who, in a dream of night, *would* fly
But *cannot* from a danger nigh.

What tho' the moon—the white moon
Shed all the splendor of her noon,
Her smile is chilly—and *her* beam,
In that time of dreariness, will seem
(So like you gather in your breath)
A portrait taken after death.
And boyhood is a summer sun
Whose waning is the dreariest one—
For all we live to know is known
And all we seek to keep hath flown—
Let life, then, as the day-flower, fall
With the noon-day beauty—which is all.

I reach'd my home—my home no more—
    For all had flown who made it so.
I pass'd from out its mossy door,
    And, tho' my tread was soft and low,
A voice came from the threshold stone
Of one whom I had earlier known—
    O, I defy thee, Hell, to show
    On beds of fire that burn below,
    An humbler heart—a deeper wo.

Father, I firmly do believe—
    I *know*—for Death who comes for me
    From regions of the blest afar,
Where there is nothing to deceive,

Hath left his iron gate ajar,
 And rays of truth you cannot see
 Are flashing thro' Eternity——
I do believe that Eblis hath
A snare in every human path—
Else how, when in the holy grove
I wandered of the idol, Love,
Who daily scents his snowy wings
With incense of burnt offerings
From the most unpolluted things,
Whose pleasant bowers are yet so riven
Above with trellic'd rays from Heaven
No mote may shun—no tiniest fly—
The light'ning of his eagle eye—
How was it that Ambition crept,
 Unseen, amid the revels there,
Till growing bold, he laughed and leapt
 In the tangles of Love's very hair?

Song

I saw thee on thy bridal day—
 When a burning blush came o'er thee,
Though happiness around thee lay,
 The world all love before thee:

And in thine eye a kindling light
 (Whatever it might be)
Was all on Earth my aching sight
 Of Loveliness could see.

That blush, perhaps, was maiden shame—
    As such it well may pass—
Though its glow hath raised a fiercer flame
    In the breast of him, alas!

Who saw thee on that bridal day,
    When that deep blush *would* come o'er thee,
Though happiness around thee lay,
    The world all love before thee.

Dreams

Oh! that my young life were a lasting dream!
My spirit not awak'ning till the beam
Of an Eternity should bring the morrow:
Yes! tho' that long dream were of hopeless sorrow,
'Twere better than the dull reality
Of waking life to him whose heart shall be,
And hath been ever, on the chilly earth,
A chaos of deep passion from his birth!

But should it be—that dream eternally
Continuing—as dreams have been to me
In my young boyhood—should it thus be given,
'Twere folly still to hope for higher Heaven!
For I have revell'd, when the sun was bright
In the summer sky; in dreamy fields of light,
And left unheedingly my very heart

In climes of mine imagining—apart
From mine own home, with beings that have been
Of mine own thought—what more could I have seen?

'Twas once and *only* once and the wild hour
From my remembrance shall not pass—some power
Or spell had bound me—'twas the chilly wind
Came o'er me in the night and left behind
Its image on my spirit, or the moon
Shone on my slumbers in her lofty noon
Too coldly—or the stars—howe'er it was
That dream was as that night wind—let it pass.

I have been happy—tho' but in a dream.
I have been happy—and I love the theme—
Dreams! in their vivid colouring of life—
As in that fleeting, shadowy, misty strife
Of semblance with reality which brings
To the delirious eye more lovely things
Of Paradise and Love—and all our own!
Than young Hope in his sunniest hour hath known.

Spirits of the Dead

I

Thy soul shall find itself alone
'Mid dark thoughts of the gray tomb-stone—
Not one, of all the crowd, to pry
Into thine hour of secrecy:

II

Be silent in that solitude,
   Which is not loneliness—for then
The spirits of the dead who stood
   In life before thee are again
In death around thee—and their will
Shall overshadow thee: be still.

III

The night—tho' clear—shall frown—
And the stars shall look not down,
From their high thrones in the heaven,
With light like Hope to mortals given—
But their red orbs, without beam,
To thy weariness shall seem
As a burning and a fever
Which would cling to thee for ever.

IV

Now are thoughts thou shalt not banish—
Now are visions ne'er to vanish—
From thy spirit shall they pass
No more—like dew-drop from the grass.

V

The breeze—the breath of God—is still—
And the mist upon the hill
Shadowy—shadowy—yet unbroken,
Is a symbol and a token—
How it hangs upon the trees,
A mystery of mysteries!—

Evening Star

'Twas noontide of summer,
   And mid-time of night;
And stars, in their orbits,
   Shone pale, thro' the light
Of the brighter, cold moon,
   'Mid planets her slaves,
Herself in the Heavens,
   Her beam on the waves.
   I gaz'd awhile
   On her cold smile;
Too cold—too cold for me—
   There pass'd, as a shroud,
   A fleecy cloud,
And I turn'd away to thee,
   Proud Evening Star,
   In thy glory afar,
And dearer thy beam shall be;
   For joy to my heart
   Is the proud part
Thou bearest in Heav'n at night,
   And more I admire
   Thy distant fire,
Than that colder, lowly light.

"Stanzas"

How often we forget all time, when lone
Admiring Nature's universal throne;
Her woods—her wilds—her mountains—the intense
Reply of HERS to OUR intelligence!

1

In youth have I known one with whom the Earth
In secret communing held—as he with it,
In day light, and in beauty from his birth:
Whose fervid, flick'ring torch of life was lit
From the sun and stars, whence he had drawn forth
A passionate light—such for his spirit was fit—
And yet that spirit knew—not in the hour
Of its own fervor—what had o'er it power.

2

Perhaps it may be that my mind is wrought
To a ferver by the moon beam that hangs o'er,
But I will half believe that wild light fraught
With more of sov'reignty than ancient lore
Hath ever told—or is it of a thought
The unembodied essence, and no more
That with a quick'ning spell doth o'er us pass
As dew of the night-time, o'er the summer grass?

3

Doth o'er us pass, when, as th' expanding eye
To the lov'd object—so the tear to the lid
Will start, which lately slept in apathy?

And yet it need not be—(that object) hid
From us in life—but common—which doth lie
Each hour before us—but *then* only bid
With a strange sound, as of a harp-string broken
T' awake us—'Tis a symbol and a token.

4

Of what in other worlds shall be—and giv'n
In beauty by our God, to those alone
Who otherwise would fall from life and Heav'n
Drawn by their heart's passion, and that tone,
That high tone of the spirit which hath striv'n
Tho' not with Faith—with godlines—whose throne
With desp'rate energy 't hath beaten down;
Wearing its own deep feeling as a crown.

A Dream

In visions of the dark night
   I have dreamed of joy departed—
But a waking dream of life and light
   Hath left me broken-hearted.

Ah! what is not a dream by day
   To him whose eyes are cast
On things around him with a ray
   Turned back upon the past?

That holy dream—that holy dream,
   While all the world were chiding,

Hath cheered me as a lovely beam
  A lonely spirit guiding.

What though that light, thro' storm and night,
  So trembled from afar—
What could there be more purely bright
  In Truth's day-star?

"The Happiest Day"

The happiest day—the happiest hour
  My sear'd and blighted heart hath known,
The highest hope of pride, and power,
  I feel hath flown.

Of power! said I? yes! such I ween
  But they have vanish'd long alas!
The visions of my youth have been—
  But let them pass.

And, pride, what have I now with thee?
  Another brow may ev'n inherit
The venom thou hast pour'd on me—
  Be still my spirit.

The happiest day—the happiest hour
  Mine eyes shall see—have ever seen
The brightest glance of pride and power
  I feel—have been:

But were that hope of pride and power
    Now offer'd, with the pain
Ev'n *then* I felt—that brightest hour
    I would not live again:

For on its wing was dark alloy
    And as it flutter'd—fell
An essence—powerful to destroy
    A soul that knew it well.

The Lake—To ——

In spring of youth it was my lot
To haunt of the wide world a spot
The which I could not love the less—
So lovely was the loneliness
Of a wild lake, with black rock bound,
And the tall pines that towered around.

But when the Night had thrown her pall
Upon that spot, as upon all,
And the mystic wind went by
Murmuring in melody—
Then—ah then I would awake
To the terror of the lone lake.

Yet that terror was not fright,
But a tremulous delight—
A feeling not the jewelled mine

Could teach or bribe me to define—
Nor Love—although the Love were thine.

Death was in that poisonous wave,
And in its gulf a fitting grave
For him who thence could solace bring
To his lone imagining—
Whose solitary soul could make
An Eden of that dim lake.

Sonnet—To Science

Science! true daughter of Old Time thou art!
    Who alterest all things with thy peering eyes.
Why preyest thou thus upon the poet's heart,
    Vulture, whose wings are dull realities?
How should he love thee? or how deem thee wise,
    Who wouldst not leave him in his wandering
To seek for treasure in the jewelled skies,
    Albeit he soared with an undaunted wing?
Hast thou not dragged Diana from her car?
    And driven the Hamadryad from the wood
To seek a shelter in some happier star?
    Hast thou not torn the Naiad from her flood,
The Elfin from the green grass, and from me
The summer dream beneath the tamarind tree?

Al Aaraaf*

PART I

O! nothing earthly save the ray
(Thrown back from flowers) of Beauty's eye,
As in those gardens where the day
Springs from the gems of Circassy—
O! nothing earthly save the thrill
Of melody in woodland rill—
Or (music of the passion-hearted)
Joy's voice so peacefully departed
That like the murmur in the shell,
Its echo dwelleth and will dwell—
Oh, nothing of the dross of ours—
Yet all the beauty—all the flowers
That list our Love, and deck our bowers—
Adorn yon world afar, afar—
The wandering star.

'Twas a sweet time for Nesace—for there
Her world lay lolling on the golden air,
Near four bright suns—a temporary rest—
An oasis in desert of the blest.
Away—away—'mid seas of rays that roll
Empyrean splendor o'er th' unchained soul—
The soul that scarce (the billows are so dense)
Can struggle to its destin'd eminence—
To distant spheres, from time to time, she rode,

* A star was discovered by Tycho Brahe which appeared suddenly in the heavens—attained, in a few days, a brilliancy surpassing that of Jupiter—then as suddenly disappeared, and has never been seen since.

And late to ours, the favour'd one of God—
But, now, the ruler of an anchor'd realm,
She throws aside the sceptre—leaves the helm,
And, amid incense and high spiritual hymns,
Laves in quadruple light her angel limbs.

Now happiest, loveliest in yon lovely Earth,
Whence sprang the "Idea of Beauty" into birth,
(Falling in wreaths thro' many a startled star,
Like woman's hair 'mid pearls, until, afar,
It lit on hills Achaian, and there dwelt)
She look'd into Infinity—and knelt.
Rich clouds, for canopies, about her curled—
Fit emblems of the model of her world—
Seen but in beauty—not impeding sight
Of other beauty glittering thro' the light—
A wreath that twined each starry form around,
And all the opal'd air in color bound.

All hurriedly she knelt upon a bed
Of flowers: of lilies such as rear'd the head
*On the fair Capo Deucato, and sprang
So eagerly around about to hang
Upon the flying footsteps of—deep pride—
†Of her who lov'd a mortal—and so died.
The Sephalica, budding with young bees,
Uprear'd its purple stem around her knees:
‡And gemmy flower, of Trebizond misnam'd—

* On Santa Maura—olim Deucadia.
† Sappho.
‡ This flower is much noticed by Lewenhoeck and Tournefort. The bee, feeding upon its blossom, becomes intoxicated.

Inmate of highest stars, where erst it sham'd
All other loveliness: its honied dew
(The fabled nectar that the heathen knew)
Deliriously sweet, was dropp'd from Heaven,
And fell on gardens of the unforgiven
In Trebizond—and on a sunny flower
So like its own above that, to this hour,
It still remaineth, torturing the bee
With madness, and unwonted reverie:
In Heaven, and all its environs, the leaf
And blossom of the fairy plant, in grief
Disconsolate linger—grief that hangs her head,
Repenting follies that full long have fled,
Heaving her white breast to the balmy air,
Like guilty beauty, chasten'd, and more fair:
Nyctanthes too, as sacred as the light
She fears to perfume, perfuming the night:
*And Clytia pondering between many a sun,
While pettish tears adown her petals run:
†And that aspiring flower that sprang on Earth—
And died, ere scarce exalted into birth,
Bursting its odorous heart in spirit to wing

* Clytia—The Chrysanthemum Peruvianum, or, to employ a better-
known term, the turnsol—which turns continually towards the sun,
covers itself, like Peru, the country from which it comes, with dewy
clouds which cool and refresh its flowers during the most violent heat
of the day—*B. de St. Pierre*.

† There is cultivated in the king's garden at Paris, a species of serpentine
aloes without prickles, whose large and beautiful flower exhales a strong
odour of the vanilla, during the time of its expansion, which is very short.
It does not blow till towards the month of July—you then perceive it
gradually open its petals—expand them—fade and die.—*St. Pierre*.

Its way to Heaven, from garden of a king:
*And Valisnerian lotus thither flown
From struggling with the waters of the Rhone:
†And thy most lovely purple perfume, Zante!
Isola d'oro!—Fior di Levante!
‡And the Nelumbo bud that floats for ever
With Indian Cupid down the holy river—
Fair flowers, and fairy! to whose care is given
§To bear the Goddess' song, in odors, up to Heaven:

"Spirit! that dwellest where,
    In the deep sky,
The terrible and fair,
    In beauty vie!
Beyond the line of blue—
    The boundary of the star
Which turneth at the view
    Of thy barrier and thy bar—
Of the barrier overgone
    By the comets who were cast
From their pride, and from their throne
    To be drudges till the last—
    To be carriers of fire

* There is found, in the Rhone, a beautiful lily of the Valisnerian kind. Its stem will stretch to the length of three or four feet—thus preserving its head above water in the swellings of the river.

† The Hyacinth.

‡ It is a fiction of the Indians, that Cupid was first seen floating in one of these down the river Ganges—and that he still loves the cradle of his childhood.

§ And golden vials full of odors which are the prayers of the saints. —*Rev. St. John.*

(The red fire of their heart)
　With speed that may not tire
　　And with pain that shall not part—
Who livest—*that* we know—
　In Eternity—we feel—
But the shadow of whose brow
　What spirit shall reveal?
Tho' the beings whom thy Nesace,
　Thy messenger hath known
Have dream'd for thy Infinity
*A model of their own—
Thy will is done, Oh, God!
　The star hath ridden high
Thro' many a tempest, but she rode
　Beneath thy burning eye;

* The Humanitarians held that God was to be understood as having really a human form.—*Vide Clarke's Sermons*, vol. 1, page 26, fol. edit.

The drift of Milton's argument, leads him to employ language which would appear, at first sight, to verge upon their doctrine; but it will be seen immediately, that he guards himself against the charge of having adopted one of the most ignorant errors of the dark ages of the church.—*Dr. Sumner's Notes on Milton's Christian Doctrine.*

This opinion, in spite of many testimonies to the contrary, could never have been very general. Andeus, a Syrian of Mesopotamia, was condemned for the opinion, as heretical. He lived in the beginning of the fourth century. His disciples were called Anthropmorphites.—*Vide Du Pin.*

Among Milton's minor poems are these lines:—

　　Dicite sacrorum præsides nemorum Deæ, &c.
　　Quis ille primus cujus ex imagine
　　Natura solers finxit humanum genus?
　　Eternus, incorruptus, æquævus polo,
　　Unusque et universus exemplar Dei.—And afterwards,
　　Non cui profundum Cæcitas lumen dedit
　　Dircæus augur vidit hunc alto sinu, &c.

And here, in thought, to thee—
    In thought that can alone
Ascend thy empire and so be
    A partner of thy throne—
*By winged Fantasy,
    My embassy is given,
Till secrecy shall knowledge be
    In the environs of Heaven."

She ceas'd—and buried then her burning cheek
Abash'd, amid the lilies there, to seek
A shelter from the fervour of His eye;
For the stars trembled at the Deity.
She stirr'd not—breath'd not—for a voice was there
How solemnly pervading the calm air!
A sound of silence on the startled ear
Which dreamy poets name "the music of the sphere."
Ours is a world of words: Quiet we call
"Silence"—which is the merest word of all.
All Nature speaks, and ev'n ideal things
Flap shadowy sounds from visionary wings—
But ah! not so when, thus, in realms on high
The eternal voice of God is passing by,
And the red winds are withering in the sky!

    †"What tho' in worlds which sightless cycles run,
Link'd to a little system, and one sun—

---

* Seltsamen Tochter Jovis
  Seinem Schosskinde
  Der Phantasie.—*Göethe*.
† Sightless—too small to be seen. — *Legge*.

Where all my love is folly and the crowd
Still think my terrors but the thunder cloud,
The storm, the earthquake, and the ocean-wrath—
(Ah! will they cross me in my angrier path?)
What tho' in worlds which own a single sun
The sands of Time grow dimmer as they run,
Yet thine is my resplendency, so given
To bear my secrets thro' the upper Heaven.
Leave tenantless thy crystal home, and fly,
With all thy train, athwart the moony sky—
*Apart—like fire-flies in Sicilian night,
And wing to other worlds another light!
Divulge the secrets of thy embassy
To the proud orbs that twinkle—and so be
To ev'ry heart a barrier and a ban
Lest the stars totter in the guilt of man!"

   Up rose the maiden in the yellow night,
The single-mooned eve!—on Earth we plight
Our faith to one love—and one moon adore—
The birth-place of young Beauty had no more.
As sprang that yellow star from downy hours
Up rose the maiden from her shrine of flowers;
And bent o'er sheeny mountain and dim plain
†Her way—but left not yet her Therasæan reign.

---

  * I have often noticed a peculiar movement of the fire-flies;—they
will collect in a body and fly off, from a common centre, into innumer-
able radii.

  † Therasæa, or Therasea, the island mentioned by Seneca, which, in a
moment, arose from the sea to the eyes of astonished mariners.

PART II

High on a mountain of enamell'd head—
Such as the drowsy shepherd on his bed
Of giant pasturage lying at his ease,
Raising his heavy eyelid, starts and sees
With many a mutter'd "hope to be forgiven"
What time the moon is quadrated in Heaven—
Of rosy head, that towering far away
Into the sunlit ether, caught the ray
Of sunken suns at eve—at noon of night,
While the moon danc'd with the fair stranger light—
Uprear'd upon such height arose a pile
Of gorgeous columns on th' unburthen'd air,
Flashing from Parian marble that twin smile
Far down upon the wave that sparkled there,
And nursled the young mountain in its lair.
*Of molten stars their pavement, such as fall
Thro' the ebon air, besilvering the pall
Of their own dissolution, while they die—
Adorning then the dwellings of the sky.
A dome, by linked light from Heaven let down,
Sat gently on these columns as a crown—
A window of one circular diamond, there,
Look'd out above into the purple air,
And rays from God shot down that meteor chain
And hallow'd all the beauty twice again,
Save when, between th' Empyrean and that ring,
Some eager spirit flapp'd his dusky wing.
But on the pillars Seraph eyes have seen

* Some star which, from the ruin'd roof
  Of shak'd Olympus, by mischance, did fall.—*Milton.*

The dimness of this world: that greyish green
That Nature loves the best for Beauty's grave
Lurk'd in each cornice, round each architrave—
And every sculptur'd cherub thereabout
That from his marble dwelling peeréd out,
Seem'd earthly in the shadow of his niche—
Achaian statues in a world so rich?
*Friezes from Tadmor and Persepolis—
From Balbec, and the stilly, clear abyss
†Of beautiful Gomorrah! O, the wave
Is now upon thee—but too late to save!

Sound loves to revel in a summer night:
Witness the murmur of the grey twilight
‡That stole upon the ear, in Eyraco,
Of many a wild star-gazer long ago—
That stealeth ever on the ear of him
Who, musing, gazeth on the distance dim,

---

* Voltaire, in speaking of Persepolis, says, "Je connois bien l'admira-
tion qu'inspirent ces ruines—mais un palais erigé au pied d'une chaine
des rochers sterils—peut il être un chef d'œuvre des arts!"

† "Oh! the wave"—Ula Deguisi is the Turkish appellation; but, on its
own shores, it is called Bahar Loth, or Almotanah. There were un-
doubtedly more than two cities engulphed in the "dead sea." In the val-
ley of Siddim were five—Adrah, Zeboin, Zoar, Sodom and Gomorrah.
Stephen of Byzantium mentions eight, and Strabo thirteen, (en-
gulphed)—but the last is out of all reason.

It is said, [Tacitus, Strabo, Josephus, Daniel of St. Saba, Nau, Maun-
drell, Troilo, D'Arvieux] that after an excessive drought, the vestiges of
columns, walls, &c. are seen above the surface. At *any* season, such re-
mains may be discovered by looking down into the transparent lake,
and at such distances as would argue the existence of many settlements
in the space now usurped by the 'Asphaltites.'

‡ Eyraco—Chaldea.

And sees the darkness coming as a cloud—
*Is not its form—its voice—most palpable and loud?

But what is this?—it cometh—and it brings
A music with it—'tis the rush of wings—
A pause—and then a sweeping, falling strain
And Nesace is in her halls again.
From the wild energy of wanton haste
    Her cheeks were flushing, and her lips apart;
And zone that clung around her gentle waist
    Had burst beneath the heaving of her heart.
Within the centre of that hall to breathe
She paus'd and panted, Zanthe! all beneath,
The fairy light that kiss'd her golden hair
And long'd to rest, yet could but sparkle there!

†Young flowers were whispering in melody
To happy flowers that night—and tree to tree;
Fountains were gushing music as they fell
In many a star-lit grove, or moon-lit dell;
Yet silence came upon material things—
Fair flowers, bright waterfalls and angel wings—
And sound alone that from the spirit sprang
Bore burthen to the charm the maiden sang:

" 'Neath blue-bell or streamer—
    Or tufted wild spray

---

* I have often thought I could distinctly hear the sound of the darkness as it stole over the horizon.

† Fairies use flowers for their charactery.—*Merry Wives of Windsor*.

That keeps, from the dreamer,
    *The moonbeam away—
Bright beings! that ponder,
    With half closing eyes,
On the stars which your wonder
    Hath drawn from the skies,
Till they glance thro' the shade, and
    Come down to your brow
Like——eyes of the maiden
    Who calls on you now—
Arise! from your dreaming
    In violet bowers,
To duty beseeming
    These star-litten hours—
And shake from your tresses
    Encumber'd with dew
The breath of those kisses
    That cumber them too—
(O! how, without you, Love!
    Could angels be blest?)
Those kisses of true love
    That lull'd ye to rest!
Up!—shake from your wing
    Each hindering thing:
The dew of the night—
    It would weigh down your flight;

* In Scripture is this passage—"The sun shall not harm thee by day, nor the moon by night." It is perhaps not generally known that the moon, in Egypt, has the effect of producing blindness to those who sleep with the face exposed to its rays, to which circumstance the passage evidently alludes.

And true love caresses—
    O! leave them apart!
They are light on the tresses,
    But lead on the heart.

Ligeia! Ligeia!
    My beautiful one!
Whose harshest idea
    Will to melody run,
O! is it thy will
    On the breezes to toss?
Or, capriciously still,
    *Like the lone Albatross,
Incumbent on night
    (As she on the air)
To keep watch with delight
    On the harmony there?

Ligeia! wherever
    Thy image may be,
No magic shall sever
    Thy music from thee.
Thou hast bound many eyes
    In a dreamy sleep—
But the strains still arise
    Which *thy* vigilance keep—
The sound of the rain
    Which leaps down to the flower,
And dances again

* The Albatross is said to sleep on the wing.

In the rhythm of the shower—
*The murmur that springs
  From the growing of grass
Are the music of things—
  But are modell'd, alas!—
Away, then my dearest,
  O! hie thee away
To springs that lie clearest
  Beneath the moon-ray—
To lone lake that smiles,
  In its dream of deep rest,
At the many star-isles
  That enjewel its breast—
Where wild flowers, creeping,
  Have mingled their shade,
On its margin is sleeping
  Full many a maid—
Some have left the cool glade, and
  †Have slept with the bee—
Arouse them my maiden,

---

* I met with this idea in an old English tale, which I am now unable
to obtain and quote from memory:—"The verie essence and, as it were,
springe-heade and originc of all musiche is the verie pleasaunte sounde
which the trees of the forest do make when they growe."

† The wild bee will not sleep in the shade if there be moonlight.
The rhyme in this verse, as in one about sixty lines before, has an ap-
pearance of affectation. It is, however, imitated from Sir W. Scott, or
rather from Claud Halcro—in whose mouth I admired its effect:

　　　O! were there an island,
　　　　Tho' ever so wild
　　　Where woman might smile, and
　　　　No man be beguil'd, &c.

On moorland and lea—
Go! breathe on their slumber,
    All softly in ear,
The musical number
    They slumber'd to hear—
For what can awaken
    An angel so soon
Whose sleep hath been taken
    Beneath the cold moon,
As the spell which no slumber
    Of witchery may test,
The rhythmical number
    Which lull'd him to rest?"

Spirits in wing, and angels to the view,
A thousand seraphs burst th' Empyrean thro',
Young dreams still hovering on their drowsy flight—
Seraphs in all but "Knowledge," the keen light
That fell, refracted, thro' thy bounds, afar
O Death! from eye of God upon that star:
Sweet was that error—sweeter still that death—
Sweet was that error—ev'n with *us* the breath
Of Science dims the mirror of our joy—
To them 'twere the Simoom, and would destroy—
For what (to them) availeth it to know
That Truth is Falsehood—or that Bliss is Woe?
Sweet was their death—with them to die was rife
With the last ecstasy of satiate life—
Beyond that death no immortality—
But sleep that pondereth and is not "to be"—

And there—oh! may my weary spirit dwell—
*Apart from Heaven's Eternity—and yet how far from
    Hell!

What guilty spirit, in what shrubbery dim,
Heard not the stirring summons of that hymn?
But two: they fell: for Heaven no grace imparts
To those who hear not for their beating hearts.
A maiden-angel and her seraph-lover—
O! where (and ye may seek the wide skies over)
Was Love, the blind, near sober Duty known?
†Unguided Love hath fallen—'mid "tears of perfect
    moan."

He was a goodly spirit—he who fell:
A wanderer by moss-y-mantled well—
A gazer on the lights that shine above—

* With the Arabians there is a medium between Heaven and Hell,
where men suffer no punishment, but yet do not attain that tranquil
and even happiness which they suppose to be characteristic of heavenly
enjoyment.

        Un no rompido sueno—
        Un dia puro—allegre—libre
        Quiera—
        Libre de amor—de zelo—
        De odio—de esperanza—de rezelo.—*Luis Ponce de Leon.*

Sorrow is not excluded from "Al Aaraaf," but it is that sorrow which
the living love to cherish for the dead, and which, in some minds, re-
sembles the delirium of opium. The passionate excitement of Love and
the buoyancy of spirit attendant upon intoxication are its less holy
pleasures—the price of which, to those souls who make choice of "Al
Aaraaf" as their residence after life, is final death and annihilation.

† There be tears of perfect moan
  Wept for thee in Helicon.—*Milton.*

A dreamer in the moonbeam by his love:
What wonder? for each star is eye-like there,
And looks so sweetly down on Beauty's hair—
And they, and ev'ry mossy spring were holy
To his love-haunted heart and melancholy.
The night had found (to him a night of wo)
Upon a mountain crag, young Angelo—
Beetling it bends athwart the solemn sky,
And scowls on starry worlds that down beneath it lie.
Here sate he with his love—his dark eye bent
With eagle gaze along the firmament:
Now turn'd it upon her—but ever then
It trembled to the orb of EARTH again.

"Ianthe, dearest, see! how dim that ray!
How lovely 'tis to look so far away!
She seem'd not thus upon that autumn eve
I left her gorgeous halls—nor mourn'd to leave.
That eve—that eve—I should remember well—
The sun-ray dropp'd, in Lemnos, with a spell
On th' Arabesque carving of a gilded hall
Wherein I sate, and on the draperied wall—
And on my eye-lids—O the heavy light!
How drowsily it weigh'd them into night!
On flowers, before, and mist, and love they ran
With Persian Saadi in his Gulistan:
But O that light!—I slumber'd—Death, the while,
Stole o'er my senses in that lovely isle
So softly that no single silken hair
Awoke that slept—or knew that he was there.

The last spot of Earth's orb I trod upon
*Was a proud temple call'd the Parthenon—
More beauty clung around her column'd wall
†Than ev'n thy glowing bosom beats withal,
And when old Time my wing did disenthral
Thence sprang I—as the eagle from his tower,
And years I left behind me in an hour.
What time upon her airy bounds I hung
One half the garden of her globe was flung
Unrolling as a chart unto my view—
Tenantless cities of the desert too!
Ianthe, beauty crowded on me then,
And half I wish'd to be again of men."

"My Angelo! and why of them to be?
A brighter dwelling-place is here for thee—
And greener fields than in yon world above,
And woman's loveliness—and passionate love."

"But, list, Ianthe! when the air so soft
‡Fail'd, as my pennon'd spirit leapt aloft,
Perhaps my brain grew dizzy—but the world
I left so late was into chaos hurl'd—
Sprang from her station, on the winds apart,
And roll'd, a flame, the fiery Heaven athwart.
Methought, my sweet one, then I ceased to soar
And fell—not swiftly as I rose before,

* It was entire in 1687—the most elevated spot in Athens.
† Shadowing more beauty in their airy brows
   Than have the white breasts of the Queen of Love.—*Marlowe*.
‡ Pennon—for pinion.—*Milton*.

But with a downward, tremulous motion thro'
Light, brazen rays, this golden star unto!
Nor long the measure of my falling hours,
For nearest of all stars was thine to ours—
Dread star! that came, amid a night of mirth,
A red Dædalion on the timid Earth."

"We came—and to thy Earth—but not to us
Be given our lady's bidding to discuss:
We came, my love; around, above, below,
Gay fire-fly of the night we come and go,
Nor ask a reason save the angel-nod
She grants to us, as granted by her God—
But, Angelo, than thine grey Time unfurl'd
Never his fairy wing o'er fairier world!
Dim was its little disk, and angel eyes
Alone could see the phantom in the skies,
When first Al Aaraaf knew her course to be
Headlong thitherward o'er the starry sea—
But when its glory swell'd upon the sky,
As glowing Beauty's bust beneath man's eye,
We paus'd before the heritage of men,
And thy star trembled—as doth Beauty then!"

Thus, in discourse, the lovers whiled away
The night that waned and waned and brought no day.
They fell: for Heaven to them no hope imparts
Who hear not for the beating of their hearts.

Romance

Romance, who loves to nod and sing,
With drowsy head and folded wing,
Among the green leaves as they shake
Far down within some shadowy lake,
To me a painted paroquet
Hath been—a most familiar bird—
Taught me my alphabet to say—
To lisp my very earliest word
While in the wild wood I did lie,
A child—with a most knowing eye.

Of late, eternal Condor years
So shake the very Heaven on high
With tumult as they thunder by,
I have no time for idle cares
Through gazing on the unquiet sky.
And when an hour with calmer wings
Its down upon my spirit flings—
That little time with lyre and rhyme
To while away—forbidden things!
My heart would feel to be a crime
Unless it trembled with the strings.

To ——

The bowers whereat, in dreams, I see
    The wantonest singing birds,
Are lips—and all thy melody
    Of lip-begotten words—

Thine eyes, in Heaven of heart enshrined
    Then desolately fall,
O God! on my funereal mind
    Like starlight on a pall—

Thy heart—*thy* heart!—I wake and sigh,
    And sleep to dream till day
Of the truth that gold can never buy—
    Of the baubles that it may.

To the River——

Fair river! in thy bright, clear flow
    Of crystal, wandering water,
Thou art an emblem of the glow
        Of beauty—the unhidden heart—
        The playful maziness of art
    In old Alberto's daughter;

But when within thy wave she looks—
    Which glistens then, and trembles—
Why, then, the prettiest of brooks
    Her worshipper resembles;
For in his heart, as in thy stream,
    Her image deeply lies—
His heart which trembles at the beam
    Of her soul-searching eyes.

To ——

I heed not that my earthly lot
    Hath—little of Earth in it—
That years of love have been forgot
    In the hatred of a minute:—
I mourn not that the desolate
    Are happier, sweet, than I,
But that *you* sorrow for *my* fate
    Who am a passer by.

Fairy-Land

Dim vales—and shadowy floods—
And cloudy-looking woods,
Whose forms we can't discover
For the tears that drip all over
Huge moons there wax and wane—
Again—again—again—
Every moment of the night—
Forever changing places—
And they put out the star-light
With the breath from their pale faces.
About twelve by the moon-dial
One more filmy than the rest
(A kind which, upon trial,
They have found to be the best)
Comes down—still down—and down
With its centre on the crown
Of a mountain's eminence,

While its wide circumference
In easy drapery falls
Over hamlets, over halls,
Wherever they may be—
O'er the strange woods—o'er the sea—
Over spirits on the wing—
Over every drowsy thing—
And buries them up quite
In a labyrinth of light—
And then, how deep!—O, deep!
Is the passion of their sleep.
In the morning they arise,
And their moony covering
Is soaring in the skies,
With the tempests as they toss,
Like——almost any thing—
Or a yellow Albatross.
They use that moon no more
For the same end as before—
Videlicet a tent—
Which I think extravagant:
Its atomies, however,
Into a shower dissever,
Of which those butterflies,
Of Earth, who seek the skies,
And so come down again
(Never-contented things!)
Have brought a specimen
Upon their quivering wings.

"Alone"

From childhood's hour I have not been
As others were—I have not seen
As others saw—I could not bring
My passions from a common spring—
From the same source I have not taken
My sorrow—I could not awaken
My heart to joy at the same tone—
And all I lov'd—*I* lov'd alone—
Then—in my childhood—in the dawn
Of a most stormy life—was drawn
From ev'ry depth of good and ill
The mystery which binds me still—
From the torrent, or the fountain—
From the red cliff of the mountain—
From the sun that 'round me roll'd
In its autumn tint of gold—
From the lightning in the sky
As it pass'd me flying by—
From the thunder, and the storm—
And the cloud that took the form
(When the rest of Heaven was blue)
Of a demon in my view—

"To Isaac Lea"

It was my choice or chance or curse
To adopt the cause for better or worse
And with my worldly goods and wit
And soul and body worship it.

Elizabeth

Elizabeth—it surely is most fit
(Logic and common usage so commanding)
In thy own book that *first* thy name be writ,
Zeno* and other sages notwithstanding;
And *I* have other reasons for so doing
Besides my innate love of contradiction;
Each poet—*if* a poet—in pursuing
The muses thro' their bowers of Truth or Fiction,
Has studied very little of his part,
Read nothing, written less—in short's a fool
Endued with neither soul, nor sense, nor art,
Being ignorant of one important rule,
Employed in even the theses of the school—
Called—I forget the heathenish Greek name—
(Called any thing, its meaning is the same)
"Always write *first* things uppermost in the heart."

* It was a saying of this philosopher "that one's own name should never appear in one's own book."

An Acrostic

Elizabeth it is in vain you say
"Love not"—thou sayest it in so sweet a way:
In vain those words from thee or L. E. L.
Zantippe's talents had enforced so well:
Ah! if that language from thy heart arise,
Breathe it less gently forth—and veil thine eyes.
Endymion, recollect, when Luna tried
To cure his love—was cured of all beside—
His folly—pride—and passion—for he died.

To Helen

Helen, thy beauty is to me
   Like those Nicéan barks of yore,
That gently, o'er a perfumed sea,
   The weary, way-worn wanderer bore
   To his own native shore.

On desperate seas long wont to roam,
   Thy hyacinth hair, thy classic face,
Thy Naiad airs have brought me home
   To the glory that was Greece,
   And the grandeur that was Rome.

Lo! in yon brilliant window-niche
   How statue-like I see thee stand,
The agate lamp within thy hand!
   Ah, Psyche, from the regions which
   Are Holy-Land!

Israfel*

In Heaven a spirit doth dwell
  "Whose heart-strings are a lute;"
None sing so wildly well
As the angel Israfel,
And the giddy stars (so legends tell)
Ceasing their hymns, attend the spell
  Of his voice, all mute.

Tottering above
  In her highest noon,
  The enamoured moon
Blushes with love,
  While, to listen, the red levin
  (With the rapid Pleiads, even,
  Which were seven,)
  Pauses in Heaven.

And they say (the starry choir
  And the other listening things)
That Israfeli's fire
Is owing to that lyre
  By which he sits and sings—
The trembling living wire
Of those unusual strings.

But the skies that angel trod,
  Where deep thoughts are a duty—

* And the angel Israfel, whose heart-strings are a lute, and who has
the sweetest voice of all God's creatures.—KORAN

Where Love's a grown-up God—
    Where the Houri glances are
Imbued with all the beauty
    Which we worship in a star.

Therefore, thou art not wrong,
    Israfeli, who despisest
An unimpassioned song;
To thee the laurels belong,
    Best bard, because the wisest!
Merrily live, and long!

The ecstasies above
    With thy burning measures suit—
Thy grief, thy joy, thy hate, thy love,
With the fervour of thy lute—
Well may the stars be mute!

Yes, Heaven is thine; but this
    Is a world of sweets and sours;
    Our flowers are merely—flowers,
And the shadow of thy perfect bliss
    Is the sunshine of ours.

If I could dwell
Where Israfel
    Hath dwelt, and he where I,
He might not sing so wildly well
    A mortal melody,
While a bolder note than this might swell
    From my lyre within the sky.

The Sleeper

At midnight, in the month of June,
I stand beneath the mystic moon.
An opiate vapour, dewy, dim,
Exhales from out her golden rim,
And, softly dripping, drop by drop,
Upon the quiet mountain top,
Steals drowsily and musically
Into the universal valley.
The rosemary nods upon the grave;
The lily lolls upon the wave;
Wrapping the fog about its breast,
The ruin moulders into rest;
Looking like Lethë, see! the lake
A conscious slumber seems to take,
And would not, for the world, awake.
All Beauty sleeps!—and lo! where lies
Irenë, with her Destinies!

Oh, lady bright! can it be right—
This window open to the night?
The wanton airs, from the tree-top,
Laughingly through the lattice drop—
The bodiless airs, a wizard rout,
Flit through thy chamber in and out,
And wave the curtain canopy
So fitfully—so fearfully—
Above the closed and fringéd lid
'Neath which thy slumb'ring soul lies hid,
That, o'er the floor and down the wall,

Like ghosts the shadows rise and fall!
Oh, lady dear, hast thou no fear?
Why and what are thou dreaming here?
Sure thou art come o'er far-off seas,
A wonder to these garden trees!
Strange is thy pallor! strange thy dress!
Strange, above all, thy length of tress,
And this all solemn silentness!

The lady sleeps! Oh, may her sleep,
Which is enduring, so be deep!
Heaven have her in its sacred keep!
This chamber changed for one more holy,
This bed for one more melancholy,
I pray to God that she may lie
Forever with unopened eye,
While the pale sheeted ghosts go by!

My love, she sleeps! Oh, may her sleep,
As it is lasting, so be deep!
Soft may the worms about her creep!
Far in the forest, dim and old,
For her may some tall vault unfold—
Some vault that oft hath flung its black
And wingéd pannels fluttering back,
Triumphant, o'er the crested palls,
Of her grand family funerals—
Some sepulchre, remote, alone,
Against whose portal she hath thrown,
In childhood, many an idle stone—
Some tomb from out whose sounding door

She ne'er shall force an echo more,
Thrilling to think, poor child of sin!
It was the dead who groaned within.

The Valley of Unrest

Once it smiled a silent dell
Where the people did not dwell;
They had gone unto the wars,
Trusting to the mild-eyed stars,
Nightly, from their azure towers,
To keep watch above the flowers,
In the midst of which all day
The red sun-light lazily lay.
Now each visitor shall confess
The sad valley's restlessness.
Nothing there is motionless—
Nothing save the airs that brood
Over the magic solitude.
Ah, by no wind are stirred those trees
That palpitate like the chill seas
Around the misty Hebrides!
Ah, by no wind those clouds are driven
That rustle through the unquiet Heaven
Uneasily, from morn till even,
Over the violets there that lie
In myriad types of the human eye—
Over the lilies there that wave
And weep above a nameless grave!

They wave:—from out their fragrant tops
Eternal dews come down in drops.
They weep:—from off their delicate stems
Perennial tears descend in gems.

The City in the Sea

Lo! Death has reared himself a throne
In a strange city lying alone
Far down within the dim West,
Where the good and the bad and the worst and the best
Have gone to their eternal rest.
There shrines and palaces and towers
(Time-eaten towers that tremble not!)
Resemble nothing that is ours.
Around, by lifting winds forgot,
Resignedly beneath the sky
The melancholy waters lie.

No rays from the holy heaven come down
On the long night-time of that town;
But light from out the lurid sea
Streams up the turrets silently—
Gleams up the pinnacles far and free—
Up domes—up spires—up kingly halls—
Up fanes—up Babylon-like walls—
Up shadowy long-forgotten bowers
Of sculptured ivy and stone flowers—

Up many and many a marvellous shrine
Whose wreathéd friezes intertwine
The viol, the violet, and the vine.

Resignedly beneath the sky
The melancholy waters lie.
So blend the turrets and shadows there
That all seem pendulous in air,
While from a proud tower in the town
Death looks gigantically down.

There open fanes and gaping graves
Yawn level with the luminous waves;
But not the riches there that lie
In each idol's diamond eye—
Not the gaily-jewelled dead
Tempt the waters from their bed;
For no ripples curl, alas!
Along that wilderness of glass—
No swellings tell that winds may be
Upon some far-off happier sea—
No heavings hint that winds have been
On seas less hideously serene.

But lo, a stir is in the air!
The wave—there is a movement there!
As if the towers had thrust aside,
In slightly sinking, the dull tide—
As if their tops had feebly given
A void within the filmy Heaven.

The waves have now a redder glow—
The hours are breathing faint and low—
And when, amid no earthly moans,
Down, down that town shall settle hence,
Hell, rising from a thousand thrones,
Shall do it reverence.

Lenore

Ah, broken is the golden bowl!—the spirit flown forever!
Let the bell toll!—a saintly soul floats on the Stygian
    river:—
And, Guy De Vere, hast *thou* no tear?—weep now or
    never more!
See! on yon drear and rigid bier low lies thy love,
    Lenore!
Come, let the burial rite be read—the funeral song be
    sung!—
An anthem for the queenliest dead that ever died so
    young—
A dirge for her the doubly dead in that she died so young.

"Wretches! ye loved her for her wealth and ye hated her
    for her pride;
And, when she fell in feeble health, ye blessed her—that
    she died:—
How *shall* the ritual then be read—the requiem how be
    sung

By you—by yours, the evil eye—by yours the slanderous
    tongue
That did to death the innocence that died and died so
    young?"

Peccavimus:—yet rave not thus! but let a Sabbath song
Go up to God so solemnly the dead may feel no wrong!
The sweet Lenore hath gone before, with Hope that
    flew beside,
Leaving thee wild for the dear child that should have
    been thy bride—
For her, the fair and debonair, that now so lowly lies,
The life upon her yellow hair, but not within her eyes—
The life still there upon her hair, the death upon her eyes.

"Avaunt!—avaunt! to friends from fiends the indignant
    ghost is riven—
From Hell unto a high estate within the utmost
    Heaven—
From moan and groan to a golden throne beside the
    King of Heaven:—
Let *no* bell toll, then, lest her soul, amid its hallowed
    mirth
Should catch the note as it doth float up from the
    damnéd Earth!
And I—tonight my heart is light:—no dirge will I upraise,
But waft the angel on her flight with a Pæan of old days!"

To One in Paradise

Thou wast that all to me, love,
  For which my soul did pine—
A green isle in the sea, love,
  A fountain and a shrine,
All wreathed with fairy fruits and flowers,
  And all the flowers were mine.

Ah, dream too bright to last!
  Ah, starry Hope! that didst arise
But to be overcast!
  A voice from out the Future cries,
"On! on!"—but o'er the Past
  (Dim gulf!) my spirit hovering lies
Mute, motionless, aghast!

For, alas! alas! with me
  The light of Life is o'er!
No more—no more—no more—
(Such language holds the solemn sea
  To the sands upon the shore)
Shall bloom the thunder-blasted tree,
  Or the stricken eagle soar!

And all my days are trances,
  And all my nightly dreams
Are where thy grey eye glances,
  And where thy footstep gleams—
In what ethereal dances,
By what eternal streams.

Hymn

At morn—at noon—at twilight dim—
Maria! thou hast heard my hymn!
In joy and wo—in good and ill—
Mother of God, be with me still!
When the Hours flew brightly by,
And not a cloud obscured the sky,
My soul, lest it should truant be,
Thy grace did guide to thine and thee;
Now, when storms of Fate o'ercast
Darkly my Present and my Past,
Let my Future radiant shine
With sweet hopes of thee and thine!

Enigma

The noblest name in Allegory's page,
The hand that traced inexorable rage;
A pleasing moralist whose page refined,
Displays the deepest knowledge of the mind;
A tender poet of a foreign tongue,
(Indited in the language that he sung.)
A bard of brilliant but unlicensed page
At once the shame and glory of our age,
The prince of harmony and stirling sense,
An ancient dramatist of eminence,
The bard that paints imagination's powers,
And him whose song revives departed hours,
Once more an ancient tragic bard recall,

In boldness of design surpassing all.
These names when rightly read, a name known
Which gathers all their glories in its own.

Serenade

So sweet the hour—so calm the time,
I feel it more than half a crime
When Nature sleeps and stars are mute,
To mar the silence ev'n with lute.
At rest on ocean's brilliant dies
An image of Elysium lies:
Seven Pleiades entranced in Heaven,
Form in the deep another seven:
Endymion nodding from above
Sees in the sea a second love:
Within the valleys dim and brown,
And on the spectral mountains' crown
The wearied light is lying down:
And earth, and stars, and sea, and sky
Are redolent of sleep, as I
Am redolent of thee and thine
Enthralling love, my Adeline.
But list, O list!—so soft and low
Thy lover's voice to night shall flow
That, scarce awake, thy soul shall deem
My words the music of a dream.
Thus, while no single sound too rude,
Upon thy slumber shall intrude,
Our thoughts, our souls—O God above!
In every deed shall mingle, love.

The Coliseum

Type of the antique Rome! Rich reliquary
Of lofty contemplation left to Time
By buried centuries of pomp and power!
At length—at length—after so many days
Of weary pilgrimage and burning thirst,
(Thirst for the springs of lore that in thee lie,)
I kneel, an altered and an humble man,
Amid thy shadows, and so drink within
My very soul thy grandeur, gloom, and glory!

Vastness! and Age! and Memories of Eld!
Silence! and Desolation! and dim Night!
I feel ye now—I feel ye in your strength—
O spells more sure than e'er Judæan king
Taught in the gardens of Gethsemane!
O charms more potent than the rapt Chaldee
Ever drew down from out the quiet stars!

Here, where a hero fell, a column falls!
Here, where the mimic eagle glared in gold,
A midnight vigil holds the swarthy bat!
Here, where the dames of Rome their gilded hair
Waved to the wind, now wave the reed and thistle!
Here, where on golden throne the monarch lolled,
Glides, spectre-like, unto his marble home,
Lit by the wan light of the horned moon,
The swift and silent lizard of the stones!

But stay! these walls—these ivy-clad arcades—
These mouldering plinths—these sad and blackened
     shafts—
These vague entablatures—this crumbling frieze—
These shattered cornices—this wreck—this ruin—
These stones—alas! these gray stones—are they all—
All of the famed, and the colossal left
By the corrosive Hours to Fate and me?

"Not all"—the Echoes answer me—"not all!
"Prophetic sounds and loud, arise forever
"From us, and from all Ruin, unto the wise,
"As melody from Memnon to the Sun.
"We rule the hearts of mightiest men—we rule
"With a despotic sway all giant minds.
"We are not impotent—we pallid stones.
"Not all our power is gone—not all our fame—
"Not all the magic of our high renown—
"Not all the wonder that encircles us—
"Not all the mysteries that in us lie—
"Not all the memories that hang upon
"And cling around about us as a garment,
"Clothing us in a robe of more than glory."

To F——s S. O——d

Thou wouldst be loved?—then let thy heart
    From its present pathway part not!
Being everything which now thou art,
    Be nothing which thou art not.

So with the world thy gentle ways,
    Thy grace, thy more than beauty,
Shall be an endless theme of praise,
    And love—a simple duty.

To F——

Beloved! amid the earnest woes
    That crowd around my earthly path—
(Drear path, alas! where grows
Not even one lonely rose)—
    My soul at least a solace hath
In dreams of thee, and therein knows
An Eden of bland repose.

And thus thy memory is to me
    Like some enchanted far-off isle
In some tumultuous sea—
Some ocean throbbing far and free
    With storms—but where meanwhile
Serenest skies continually
    Just o'er that one bright island smile.

Bridal Ballad

The ring is on my hand,
    And the wreath is on my brow;
Satins and jewels grand
Are all at my command,
    And I am happy now.

And my lord he loves me well;
    But, when first he breathed his vow,
I felt my bosom swell—
For the words rang as a knell,
And the voice seemed *his* who fell
In the battle down the dell,
    And who is happy now.

But he spoke to re-assure me,
    And he kissed my pallid brow,
While a reverie came o'er me,
And to the church-yard bore me,
And I sighed to him before me,
(Thinking him dead D'Elormie,)
    "Oh, I am happy now!"

And thus the words were spoken;
    And this the plighted vow;
And, though my faith be broken,
And, though my heart be broken,
Here is a ring, as token
    That I am happy now!—
Behold the golden token
    That *proves* me happy now!

Would God I could awaken!
    For I dream I know not how,
And my soul is sorely shaken
Lest an evil step be taken,—
Lest the dead who is forsaken
    May not be happy now.

Sonnet—To Zante

Fair isle, that from the fairest of all flowers,
  Thy gentlest of all gentle names dost take!
How many memories of what radiant hours
  At sight of thee and thine at once awake!
How many scenes of what departed bliss!
  How many thoughts of what entombéd hopes!
How many visions of a maiden that is
  No more—no more upon thy verdant slopes!
No more! alas, that magical sad sound
  Transforming all! Thy charms shall please *no more*—
Thy memory *no more!* Acc-uréed ground
  Henceforth I hold thy flower-enamelled shore,
O hyacinthine isle! O purple Zante!
  "Isola d'oro! Fior di Levante!"

The Haunted Palace

In the greenest of our valleys
  By good angels tenanted,
Once a fair and stately palace—
  Radiant palace—reared its head.
In the monarch Thought's dominion—
  It stood there!
Never seraph spread a pinion
  Over fabric half so fair!

Banners yellow, glorious, golden,
  On its roof did float and flow—

(This—all this—was in the olden
  Time long ago)
And every gentle air that dallied,
  In that sweet day,
Along the ramparts plumed and pallid,
  A wingéd odor went away.

Wanderers in that happy valley,
  Through two luminous windows, saw
Spirits moving musically,
  To a lute's well-tunéd law,
Round about a throne where, sitting,
  Porphyrogene,
In state his glory well befitting
  The ruler of the realm was seen.

And all with pearl and ruby glowing
  Was the fair palace door,
Through which came flowing, flowing, flowing,
  And sparkling evermore,
A troop of Echoes whose sweet duty
  Was but to sing,
In voices of surpassing beauty,
  The wit and wisdom of their king.

But evil things, in robes of sorrow,
  Assailed the monarch's high estate.
(Ah, let us mourn!—for never morrow
  Shall dawn upon him, desolate!)
And round about his home the glory
  That blushed and bloomed,

Is but a dim-remembered story
  Of the old-time entombed.

And travellers, now, within that valley,
  Through the encrimsoned windows see
Vast forms that move fantastically
  To a discordant melody,
While, like a ghastly rapid river,
  Through the pale door
A hideous throng rush out forever
  And laugh—but smile no more.

Sonnet—Silence

There are some qualities—some incorporate things,
  That have a double life, which thus is made
A type of that twin entity which springs
  From matter and light, evinced in solid and shade.
There is a two-fold *Silence*—sea and shore—
  Body and soul. One dwells in lonely places,
  Newly with grass o'ergrown; some solemn graces,
Some human memories and tearful lore,
Render him terrorless: his name's "No More."
He is the corporate Silence: dread him not!
  No power hath he of evil in himself;
But should some urgent fate (untimely lot!)
  Bring thee to meet his shadow (nameless elf,
That haunteth the lone regions where hath trod
No foot of man,) commend thyself to God!

The Conqueror Worm

Lo! 'tis a gala night
  Within the lonesome latter years!
An angel throng, bewinged, bedight
  In veils, and drowned in tears,
Sit in a theatre, to see
  A play of hopes and fears,
While the orchestra breathes fitfully
  The music of the spheres.

Mimes, in the form of God on high,
  Mutter and mumble low,
And hither and thither fly—
  Mere puppets they, who come and go
At bidding of vast formless things
  That shift the scenery to and fro,
Flapping from out their Condor wings
  Invisible Wo!

That motley drama—oh, be sure
  It shall not be forgot!
With its Phantom chased for evermore,
  By a crowd that seize it not,
Through a circle that ever returneth in
  To the self-same spot,
And much of Madness, and more of Sin,
  And Horror the soul of the plot.

But see, amid the mimic rout
  A crawling shape intrude!

A blood-red thing that writhes from out
  The scenic solitude!
It writhes!—it writhes!—with mortal pangs
  The mimes become its food,
And seraphs sob at vermin fangs
  In human gore imbued.

Out—out are the lights—out all!
  And, over each quivering form,
The curtain, a funeral pall,
  Comes down with the rush of a storm,
While the angels, all pallid and wan,
  Uprising, unveiling, affirm
That the play is the tragedy, "Man,"
  And its hero the Conqueror Worm.

Dream-Land

  By a route obscure and lonely,
  Haunted by ill angels only,
  Where an Eidolon, named NIGHT,
  On a black throne reigns upright,
  I have reached these lands but newly
  From an ultimate dim Thule—
From a wild weird clime that lieth, sublime,
      Out of SPACE—out of TIME.

  Bottomless vales and boundless floods,
  And chasms, and caves, and Titan woods,
  With forms that no man can discover

For the tears that drip all over;
Mountains toppling evermore
Into seas without a shore;
Seas that restlessly aspire,
Surging, unto skies of fire;
Lakes that endlessly outspread
Their lone waters—lone and dead,—
Their still waters—still and chilly
With the snows of the lolling lily.

By the lakes that thus outspread
Their lone waters, lone and dead,—
Their sad waters, sad and chilly
With the snows of the lolling lily,—
By the mountains—near the river
Murmuring lowly, murmuring ever,—
By the grey woods,—by the swamp
Where the toad and the newt encamp,—
By the dismal tarns and pools
    Where dwell the Ghouls,—
By each spot the most unholy—
In each nook most melancholy,—
There the traveller meets, aghast,
Sheeted Memories of the Past—
Shrouded forms that start and sigh
As they pass the wanderer by—
White-robed forms of friends long given,
In agony, to the Earth—and Heaven.

For the heart whose woes are legion
'Tis a peaceful, soothing region—

For the spirit that walks in shadow
'Tis—oh 'tis an Eldorado!
But the traveller, travelling through it,
May not—dare not openly view it;
Never its mysteries are exposed
To the weak human eye unclosed;
So wills its King, who hath forbid
The uplifting of the fringéd lid;
And thus the sad Soul that here passes
Beholds it but through darkened glasses.

By a route obscure and lonely,
Haunted by ill angels only,
Where an Eidolon, named NIGHT,
On a black throne reigns upright,
I have wandered home but newly
From this ultimate dim Thule.

Eulalie — A Song

I dwelt alone
In a world of moan,
And my soul was a stagnant tide,
Till the fair and gentle Eulalie became my blushing
bride—
Till the yellow-haired young Eulalie became my smiling
bride.

Ah, less—less bright
The stars of the night
Than the eyes of the radiant girl!
And never a flake
That the vapor can make
With the moon-tints of purple and pearl,
Can vie with the modest Eulalie's most unregarded curl—
Can compare with the bright-eyed Eulalie's most
humble and careless curl.

Now Doubt—now Pain
Come never again,
For her soul gives me sigh for sigh,
And all day long
Shines, bright and strong,
Astarté within the sky,
While ever to her dear Eulalie upturns her matron eye—
While ever to her young Eulalie upturns her violet eye.

The Raven

Once upon a midnight dreary, while I pondered, weak
and weary,
Over many a quaint and curious volume of forgotten
lore—
While I nodded, nearly napping, suddenly there came a
tapping,
As of some one gently rapping, rapping at my chamber
door.

" 'Tis some visiter," I muttered, "tapping at my chamber
   door—
        Only this and nothing more."

Ah, distinctly I remember it was in the bleak December;
And each separate dying ember wrought its ghost upon
   the floor.
Eagerly I wished the morrow;—vainly I had sought to
   borrow
From my books surcease of sorrow—sorrow for the lost
   Lenore—
For the rare and radiant maiden whom the angels name
   Lenore—
        Nameless *here* for evermore.

And the silken, sad, uncertain rustling of each purple
   curtain
Thrilled me—filled me with fantastic terrors never felt
   before;
So that now, to still the beating of my heart, I stood
   repeating
" 'Tis some visiter entreating entrance at my chamber
   door—
Some late visiter entreating entrance at my chamber
   door;—
        This it is and nothing more."

Presently my soul grew stronger; hesitating then no
   longer,
"Sir," said I, "or Madam, truly your forgiveness I implore;

But the fact is I was napping, and so gently you came
  rapping,
And so faintly you came tapping, tapping at my chamber
  door,
That I scarce was sure I heard you"—here I opened
  wide the door;——
      Darkness there and nothing more.

Deep into that darkness peering, long I stood there
  wondering, fearing,
Doubting, dreaming dreams no mortal ever dared to
  dream before;
But the silence was unbroken, and the stillness gave no
  token,
And the only word there spoken was the whispered
  word, "Lenore?"
This I whispered, and an echo murmured back the
  word, "Lenore!"
      Merely this and nothing more.

Back into the chamber turning, all my soul within me
  burning,
Soon again I heard a tapping somewhat louder than
  before.
"Surely," said I, "surely that is something at my window
  lattice;
Let me see, then, what thereat is, and this mystery
  explore—
Let my heart be still a moment and this mystery
  explore;—
      'Tis the wind and nothing more!"

Open here I flung the shutter, when, with many a flirt
and flutter,
In there stepped a stately Raven of the saintly days of yore;
Not the least obeisance made he; not a minute stopped
or stayed he;
But, with mien of lord or lady, perched above my
chamber door—
Perched upon a bust of Pallas just above my chamber
door—
Perched, and sat, and nothing more.

Then this ebony bird beguiling my sad fancy into
smiling,
By the grave and stern decorum of the countenance it
wore,
"Though thy crest be shorn and shaven, thou," I said,
"art sure no craven,
Ghastly grim and ancient Raven wandering from the
Nightly shore—
Tell me what thy lordly name is on the Night's
Plutonian shore!"
Quoth the Raven "Nevermore."

Much I marvelled this ungainly fowl to hear discourse
so plainly,
Though its answer little meaning—little relevancy bore;
For we cannot help agreeing that no living human being
Ever yet was blessed with seeing bird above his chamber
door—
Bird or beast upon the sculptured bust above his
chamber door,
With such name as "Nevermore."

But the Raven, sitting lonely on the placid bust, spoke
only
That one word, as if his soul in that one word he did
outpour.
Nothing farther then he uttered—not a feather then he
fluttered—
Till I scarcely more than muttered "Other friends have
flown before—
On the morrow *he* will leave me, as my Hopes have
flown before."
Then the bird said "Nevermore."

Startled at the stillness broken by reply so aptly spoken,
"Doubtless," said I, "what it utters is its only stock and
store
Caught from some unhappy master whom unmerciful
Disaster
Followed fast and followed faster till his songs one
burden bore—
Till the dirges of his Hope that melancholy burden bore
Of 'Never—nevermore.' "

But the Raven still beguiling my sad fancy into smiling,
Straight I wheeled a cushioned seat in front of bird, and
bust and door;
Then, upon the velvet sinking, I betook myself to linking
Fancy unto fancy, thinking what this ominous bird of
yore—
What this grim, ungainly, ghastly, gaunt, and ominous
bird of yore
Meant in croaking "Nevermore."

This I sat engaged in guessing, but no syllable expressing
To the fowl whose fiery eyes now burned into my
bosom's core;
This and more I sat divining, with my head at ease
reclining
On the cushion's velvet lining that the lamp-light
gloated o'er,
But whose velvet-violet lining with the lamp-light
gloating o'er,
She shall press, ah, nevermore!

Then, methought, the air grew denser, perfumed from
an unseen censer
Swung by seraphim whose foot-falls tinkled on the
tufted floor.
"Wretch," I cried, "thy God hath lent thee—by these
angels he hath sent thee
Respite—respite and nepenthe from thy memories of
Lenore;
Quaff, oh quaff this kind nepenthe and forget this lost
Lenore!"
Quoth the Raven "Nevermore."

"Prophet!" said I, "thing of evil!—prophet still, if bird
or devil!—
Whether Tempter sent, or whether tempest tossed thee
here ashore,
Desolate yet all undaunted, on this desert land
enchanted—
On this home by Horror haunted—tell me truly, I
implore—

Is there—*is* there balm in Gilead?—tell me—tell me, I
    implore!"

> Quoth the Raven "Nevermore."

"Prophet!" said I, "thing of evil!—prophet still, if bird
    or devil!
By that Heaven that bends above us—by that God we
    both adore—
Tell this soul with sorrow laden if, within the distant
    Aidenn,
It shall clasp a sainted maiden whom the angels name
    Lenore—
Clasp a rare and radiant maiden whom the angels name
    Lenore."

> Quoth the Raven "Nevermore."

"Be that word our sign of parting, bird or fiend!" I
    shrieked, upstarting—
"Get thee back into the tempest and the Night's
    Plutonian shore!
Leave no black plume as a token of that lie thy soul hath
    spoken!
Leave my loneliness unbroken!—quit the bust above my
    door!
Take thy beak from out my heart, and take thy form
    from off my door!"

> Quoth the Raven "Nevermore."

And the Raven, never flitting, still is sitting, *still* is sitting
On the pallid bust of Pallas just above my chamber
    door;

And his eyes have all the seeming of a demon's that is
      dreaming,
And the lamp-light o'er him streaming throws his
      shadow on the floor;
And my soul from out that shadow that lies floating on
      the floor
          Shall be lifted—nevermore!

A Valentine to —— —— ——

For her this rhyme is penned, whose luminous eyes,
    Brightly expressive as the twins of Lœda,
Shall find her own sweet name, that, nestling lies
    Upon the page, enwrapped from every reader.
Search narrowly the lines!—they hold a treasure
    Divine—a talisman—an amulet
That must be worn *at heart*. Search well the measure—
    The words—the syllables! Do not forget
The trivialest point, or you may lose your labor!
    And yet there is in this no Gordian knot
Which one might not undo without a sabre,
    If one could merely comprehend the plot.
Enwritten upon the leaf where now are peering
    Eyes scintillating soul, there lie *perdus*
Three eloquent words oft uttered in the hearing
    Of poets, by poets—as the name is a poet's, too.
Its letters, although naturally lying
    Like the knight Pinto—Mendez Ferdinando—
Still form a synonym for Truth.—Cease trying!
    You will not read the riddle, though you do the best
    you *can* do.

To Miss Louise Olivia Hunter

Though I turn, I fly not—
  I cannot depart;
I would try, but try not
  To release my heart.
And my hopes are dying
While, on dreams relying,
  I am spelled by art.

Thus the bright snake coiling
  'Neath the forest tree
Wins the bird, beguiling
  To come down and see:
Like that bird the lover—
Round his fate will hover
Till the blow is over
  And he sinks—like me.

To M. L. S——

Of all who hail thy presence as the morning—
Of all to whom thine absence is the night—
The blotting utterly from out high heaven
The sacred sun—of all who, weeping, bless thee
Hourly for hope—for life—ah! above all,
For the resurrection of deep-buried faith
In Truth—in Virtue—in Humanity—
Of all who, on Despair's unhallowed bed
Lying down to die, have suddenly arisen
At thy soft-murmured words, "Let there be light!"

At the soft-murmured words that were fulfilled
In the seraphic glancing of thine eyes—
Of all who owe thee most—whose gratitude
Nearest resembles worship—oh, remember
The truest—the most fervently devoted,
And think that these weak lines are written by him—
By him who, as he pens them, thrills to think
His spirit is communing with an angel's.

To —— —— ——

Not long ago, the writer of these lines,
In the mad pride of intellectuality,
Maintained "the power of words"—denied that ever
A thought arose within the human brain
Beyond the utterance of the human tongue;
And now, as if in mockery of that boast,
Two words—two foreign soft dissyllables—
Italian tones made only to be murmured
By angels dreaming in the moonlit "dew
That hangs like chains of pearl on Hermon hill"—
Have stirred from out the abysses of his heart,
Unthought-like thoughts that are the souls of thought,
Richer, far wilder, far diviner visions
Than even the seraph harper, Israfel,
Who has "the sweetest voice of all God's creatures,"
Could hope to utter. And I! my spells are broken.
The pen falls powerless from my shivering hand.
With thy dear name as text, though bidden by thee,
I cannot write—I cannot speak or think,

Alas, I cannot feel; for 'tis not feeling,
This standing motionless upon the golden
Threshold of the wide-open gate of dreams,
Gazing, entranced, adown the gorgeous vista,
And thrilling as I see upon the right,
Upon the left, and all the way along
Amid empurpled vapors, far away
To where the prospect terminates—*thee only*.

Ulalume — A Ballad

The skies they were ashen and sober;
   The leaves they were crispéd and sere—
   The leaves they were withering and sere:
It was night, in the lonesome October
   Of my most immemorial year:
It was hard by the dim lake of Auber,
   In the misty mid region of Weir:—
It was down by the dank tarn of Auber,
   In the ghoul-haunted woodland of Weir.

Here once, through an alley Titanic,
   Of cypress, I roamed with my Soul—
   Of cypress, with Psyche, my Soul.
These were days when my heart was volcanic
   As the scoriac rivers that roll—
   As the lavas that restlessly roll
Their sulphurous currents down Yaanek,
   In the ultimate climes of the Pole—
That groan as they roll down Mount Yaanek,
   In the realms of the Boreal Pole.

Our talk had been serious and sober,
But our thoughts they were palsied and sere—
Our memories were treacherous and sere;
For we knew not the month was October,
And we marked not the night of the year—
(Ah, night of all nights in the year!)
We noted not the dim lake of Auber,
(Though once we had journeyed down here)
We remembered not the dank tarn of Auber,
Nor the ghoul-haunted woodland of Weir.

And now, as the night was senescent,
And star-dials pointed to morn—
As the star-dials hinted of morn—
At the end of our path a liquescent
And nebulous lustre was born,
Out of which a miraculous crescent
Arose with a duplicate horn—
Astarte's bediamonded crescent,
Distinct with its duplicate horn.

And I said—"She is warmer than Dian;
She rolls through an ether of sighs—
She revels in a region of sighs.
She has seen that the tears are not dry on
These cheeks where the worm never dies,
And has come past the stars of the Lion,
To point us the path to the skies—
To the Lethean peace of the skies—
Come up, in despite of the Lion,
To shine on us with her bright eyes—

Come up, through the lair of the Lion,
    With love in her luminous eyes."

But Psyche, uplifting her finger,
    Said—"Sadly this star I mistrust—
    Her pallor I strangely mistrust—
Ah, hasten!—ah, let us not linger!
    Ah, fly!—let us fly!—for we must."
In terror she spoke; letting sink her
    Wings till they trailed in the dust—
In agony sobbed; letting sink her
    Plumes till they trailed in the dust—
    Till they sorrowfully trailed in the dust.

I replied—"This is nothing but dreaming.
    Let us on, by this tremulous light!
    Let us bathe in this crystalline light!
Its Sibyllic splendor is beaming
    With Hope and in Beauty to-night—
    See!—it flickers up the sky through the night!
Ah, we safely may trust to its gleaming
    And be sure it will lead us aright—
We surely may trust to a gleaming
    That cannot but guide us aright
Since it flickers up to Heaven through the night."

Thus I pacified Psyche and kissed her,
    And tempted her out of her gloom—
    And conquered her scruples and gloom;
And we passed to the end of the vista—
    But were stopped by the door of a tomb—

By the door of a legended tomb:—
And I said—"What is written, sweet sister,
   On the door of this legended tomb?"
   She replied—"Ulalume—Ulalume!—
   'T is the vault of thy lost Ulalume!"

Then my heart it grew ashen and sober
   As the leaves that were crispéd and sere—
   As the leaves that were withering and sere—
And I cried—"It was surely October,
   On *this* very night of last year,
   That I journeyed—I journeyed down here!—
   That I brought a dread burden down here—
   On this night, of all nights in the year,
   Ah, what demon hath tempted me here?
Well I know, now, this dim lake of Auber—
   This misty mid region of Weir:—
Well I know, now, this dank tarn of Auber—
   This ghoul-haunted woodland of Weir."

Said we, then—the two, then—"Ah, can it
   Have been that the woodlandish ghouls—
   The pitiful, the merciful ghouls,
To bar up our way and to ban it
   From the secret that lies in these wolds—
   From the thing that lies hidden in these wolds—
Have drawn up the spectre of a planet
   From the limbo of lunary souls—
This sinfully scintillant planet
   From the Hell of the planetary souls?"

An Enigma

"Seldom we find," says Solomon Don Dunce,
    "Half an idea in the profoundest sonnet.
Through all the flimsy things we see at once
    As easily as through a Naples bonnet—
    Trash of all trash!—how *can* a lady don it?
Yet heavier far than your Petrarchan stuff—
Owl-downy nonsense that the faintest puff
    Twirls into trunk-paper the while you con it."
And, veritably, Sol is right enough.
The general tuckermanities are arrant
Bubbles—ephemeral and *so* transparent—
    But *this* is, now,—you may depend upon it—
Stable, opaque, immortal—all by dint
Of the dear names that lie concealed within 't.

The Bells

1

    Hear the sledges with the bells—
        Silver bells!
What a world of merriment their melody foretells!
    How they tinkle, tinkle, tinkle,
        In the icy air of night!
    While the stars that oversprinkle
    All the Heavens, seem to twinkle
        With a crystalline delight;
    Keeping time, time, time,

In a sort of Runic rhyme,
To the tintinabulation that so musically wells
From the bells, bells, bells, bells,
Bells, bells, bells—
From the jingling and the tinkling of the bells.

2

Here the mellow wedding bells—
Golden bells!
What a world of happiness their harmony foretells!
Through the balmy air of night
How they ring out their delight!—
From the molten-golden notes
And all in tune,
What a liquid ditty floats
To the turtle-dove that listens while she gloats
On the moon!
Oh, from out the sounding cells
What a gush of euphony voluminously wells!
How it swells!
How it dwells
On the Future!—how it tells
Of the rapture that impels
To the swinging and the ringing
Of the bells, bells, bells!—
Of the bells, bells, bells, bells,
Bells, bells, bells—
To the rhyming and the chiming of the bells!

Hear the loud alarum bells—
　　Brazen bells!
What tale of terror, now, their turbulency tells!
　　In the startled ear of Night
　　How they scream out their affright!
　　　Too much horrified to speak,
　　　They can only shriek, shriek,
　　　　Out of tune,
In a clamorous appealing to the mercy of the fire—
In a mad expostulation with the deaf and frantic fire,
　　Leaping higher, higher, higher,
　　With a desperate desire
　　And a resolute endeavor
　　Now—now to sit, or never,
By the side of the pale-faced moon.
　　Oh, the bells, bells, bells!
　　What a tale their terror tells
　　　Of despair!
　　How they clang and clash and roar!
　　What a horror they outpour
In the bosom of the palpitating air!
　　Yet the ear, it fully knows,
　　　By the twanging
　　　And the clanging,
　　How the danger ebbs and flows:—
Yes, the ear distinctly tells,
　　　In the jangling
　　　And the wrangling,
　　How the danger sinks and swells,

By the sinking or the swelling in the anger of the bells—
      Of the bells—
   Of the bells, bells, bells, bells,
      Bells, bells, bells—
      In the clamor and the clangor of the bells.

4

      Hear the tolling of the bells—
         Iron bells!
What a world of solemn thought their monody compels!
      In the silence of the night
      How we shiver with affright
   At the melancholy meaning of the tone!
      For every sound that floats
      From the rust within their throats
         Is a groan.
      And the people—ah, the people
      They that dwell up in the steeple
         All alone,
      And who, tolling, tolling, tolling,
         In that muffled monotone,
      Feel a glory in so rolling
         On the human heart a stone—
   They are neither man nor woman—
   They are neither brute nor human,
         They are Ghouls:—
   And their king it is who tolls:—
   And he rolls, rolls, rolls, rolls
         A Pæan from the bells!
      And his merry bosom swells
         With the Pæan of the bells!

And he dances and he yells;
Keeping time, time, time,
In a sort of Runic rhyme,
 To the Pæan of the bells—
  Of the bells:—
Keeping time, time, time,
In a sort of Runic rhyme,
 To the throbbing of the bells—
Of the bells, bells, bells—
 To the sobbing of the bells:—
Keeping time, time, time,
 As he knells, knells, knells,
In a happy Runic rhyme,
 To the rolling of the bells—
Of the bells, bells, bells:—
 To the tolling of the bells—
Of the bells, bells, bells, bells,
  Bells, bells, bells—
To the moaning and the groaning of the bells.

To Helen

I saw thee once—once only—years ago:
I must not say *how* many—but *not* many.
It was a July midnight; and from out—
A full-orbed moon, that, like thine own soul, soaring,
Sought a precipitate pathway up through heaven,
There fell a silvery-silken veil of light,
With quietude, and sultriness, and slumber,
Upon the upturn'd faces of a thousand

Roses that grew in an enchanted garden,
Where no wind dared to stir, unless on tiptoe—
Fell on the upturn'd faces of these roses
That gave out, in return for the love-light,
Their odorous souls in an ecstatic death—
Fell on the upturn'd faces of these roses
That smiled and died in this parterre, enchanted
By thee, and by the poetry of thy presence.

Clad all in white, upon a violet bank
I saw thee half reclining; while the moon
Fell on the upturn'd faces of the roses,
And on thine own, upturn'd—alas, in sorrow!
Was it not Fate, that, on this July midnight—
Was it not Fate, (whose name is also Sorrow,)
That bade me pause before that garden-gate,
To breathe the incense of those slumbering roses?
No footstep stirred: the hated world all slept,
Save only thee and me. (Oh, Heaven!—oh, God!
How my heart beats in coupling those two words!)
Save only thee and me. I paused—I looked—
And in an instant all things disappeared.
(Ah, bear in mind this garden was enchanted!)
The pearly lustre of the moon went out:
The mossy banks and the meandering paths,
The happy flowers and the repining trees,
Were seen no more: the very roses' odors
Died in the arms of the adoring airs.
All—all expired save thee—save less than thou:
Save only the divine light in thine eyes—
Save but the soul in thine uplifted eyes.

I saw but them—they were the world to me.
I saw but them—saw only them for hours—
Saw only them until the moon went down.
What wild heart-histories seemed to lie enwritten
Upon those crystalline, celestial spheres!
How dark a wo! yet how sublime a hope!
How silently serene a sea of pride!
How daring an ambition! yet how deep—
How fathomless a capacity for love!

But now, at length, dear Dian sank from sight,
Into a western couch of thunder-cloud;
And thou, a ghost, amid the entombing trees
Didst glide away. *Only thine eyes remained.*
They *would not* go—they never yet have gone.
Lighting my lonely pathway home that night,
They have not left me (as my hopes have) since.
They follow me—they lead me through the years.
They are my ministers—yet I their slave.
Their office is to illumine and enkindle—
My duty, *to be saved* by their bright light,
And purified in their electric fire,
And sanctified in their elysian fire.
They fill my soul with Beauty (which is Hope,)
And are far up in Heaven—the stars I kneel to
In the sad, silent watches of my night;
While even in the meridian glare of day
I see them still—two sweetly scintillant
Venuses, unextinguished by the sun!

A Dream Within a Dream

Take this kiss upon the brow!
And, in parting from you now,
Thus much let me avow—
You are not wrong, who deem
That my days have been a dream;
Yet if Hope has flown away
In a night, or in a day,
In a vision, or in none,
Is it therefore the less *gone*?
All that we see or seem
Is but a dream within a dream.

I stand amid the roar
Of a surf-tormented shore,
And I hold within my hand
Grains of the golden sand—
How few! yet how they creep
Through my fingers to the deep,
While I weep—while I weep!
O God! can I not grasp
Them with a tighter clasp?
O God! can I not save
One from the pitiless wave?
Is *all* that we see or seem
But a dream within a dream?

For Annie

Thank Heaven! the crisis—
    The danger is past,
And the lingering illness
    Is over at last—
And the fever called "Living"
    Is conquered at last.

Sadly, I know
    I am shorn of my strength,
And no muscle I move
    As I lie at full length—
But no matter!—I feel
    I am better at length.

And I rest so composedly,
    Now, in my bed,
That any beholder
    Might fancy me dead—
Might start at beholding me,
    Thinking me dead.

The moaning and groaning,
    The sighing and sobbing,
Are quieted now,
    With that horrible throbbing
At heart:—ah, that horrible,
    Horrible throbbing!

The sickness—the nausea—
　The pitiless pain—
Have ceased, with the fever
　That maddened my brain—
With the fever called "Living"
　That burned in my brain.

And oh! of all tortures
　That torture the worst
Has abated—the terrible
　Torture of thirst
For the napthaline river
　Of Passion accurst:—
I have drank of a water
　That quenches all thirst:—

Of a water that flows,
　With a lullaby sound,
From a spring but a very few
　Feet under ground—
From a cavern not very far
　Down under ground.

And ah! let it never
　Be foolishly said
That my room it is gloomy
　And narrow my bed;
For man never slept
　In a different bed—
And, to *sleep*, you must slumber
　In just such a bed.

My tantalized spirit
    Here blandly reposes,
Forgetting, or never
    Regretting its roses—
Its old agitations
    Of myrtles and roses:

For now, while so quietly
    Lying, it fancies
A holier odor
    About it, of pansies—
A rosemary odor,
    Commingled with pansies—
With rue and the beautiful
    Puritan pansies.

And so it lies happily,
    Bathing in many
A dream of the truth
    And the beauty of Annie—
Drowned in a bath
    Of the tresses of Annie.

She tenderly kissed me,
    She fondly caressed,
And then I fell gently
    To sleep on her breast—
Deeply to sleep
    From the heaven of her breast.

When the light was extinguished,
　She covered me warm,
And she prayed to the angels
　To keep me from harm—
To the queen of the angels
　To shield me from harm.

And I lie so composedly,
　Now, in my bed,
(Knowing her love)
　That you fancy me dead—
And I rest so contentedly,
　Now in my bed,
(With her love at my breast)
　That you fancy me dead—
That you shudder to look at me,
　Thinking me dead:—

But my heart it is brighter
　Than all of the many
Stars in the sky,
　For it sparkles with Annie—
It glows with the light
　Of the love of my Annie—
With the thought of the light
　Of the eyes of my Annie.

Eldorado

Gaily bedight,
A gallant knight,
In sunshine and in shadow,
Had journeyed long,
Singing a song,
In search of Eldorado.

But he grew old—
This knight so bold—
And o'er his heart a shadow
Fell, as he found
No spot of ground
That looked like Eldorado.

And, as his strength
Failed him at length,
He met a pilgrim shadow—
'Shadow,' said he,
'Where can it be—
This land of Eldorado?'

'Over the Mountains
Of the Moon,
Down the Valley of the Shadow,
Ride, boldly ride,'
The shade replied,—
'If you seek for Eldorado!'

To My Mother

Because I feel that, in the Heavens above,
  The angels, whispering to one another,
Can find, among their burning terms of love,
  None so devotional as that of "Mother,"
Therefore by that dear name I long have called you—
  You who are more than mother unto me,
And fill my heart of hearts, where Death installed you
  In setting my Virginia's spirit free.
My mother—my own mother, who died early,
  Was but the mother of myself; but you
Are mother to the one I loved so dearly,
  And thus are dearer than the mother I knew
By that infinity with which my wife
  Was dearer to my soul than its soul-life.

Annabel Lee

It was many and many a year ago,
  In a kingdom by the sea,
That a maiden there lived whom you may know
  By the name of Annabel Lee;—
And this maiden she lived with no other thought
  Than to love and be loved by me.

She was a child and *I* was a child,
  In this kingdom by the sea,
But we loved with a love that was more than love—
  I and my Annabel Lee—
With a love that the wingéd seraphs of Heaven
  Coveted her and me.

And this was the reason that, long ago,
   In this kingdom by the sea,
A wind blew out of a cloud by night
   Chilling my Annabel Lee;
So that her high-born kinsmen came
   And bore her away from me,
To shut her up in a sepulchre
   In this kingdom by the sea.

The angels, not half so happy in Heaven,
   Went envying her and me;
Yes! that was the reason (as all men know,
   In this kingdom by the sea)
That the wind came out of the cloud, chilling
   And killing my Annabel Lee.

But our love it was stronger by far than the love
   Of those who were older than we—
   Of many far wiser than we—
And neither the angels in Heaven above
   Nor the demons down under the sea
Can ever dissever my soul from the soul
   Of the beautiful Annabel Lee:—

For the moon never beams without bringing me dreams
   Of the beautiful Annabel Lee;
And the stars never rise but I see the bright eyes
   Of the beautiful Annabel Lee;
And so, all the night-tide, I lie down by the side
Of my darling, my darling, my life and my bride
   In her sepulchre there by the sea—
   In her tomb by the side of the sea.

Scenes from "Politian"

AN UNPUBLISHED DRAMA

I

ROME.—A Hall in a Palace. Alessandra and Castiglione.

Alessandra. Thou art sad, Castiglione.
Castiglione. Sad!—not I.
Oh, I'm the happiest, happiest man in Rome!
A few days more, thou knowest, my Alessandra,
Will make thee mine. Oh, I am very happy!
Aless. Methinks thou hast a singular way of showing
Thy happiness!—what ails thee, cousin of mine?
Why didst thou sigh so deeply?
Cas. Did I sigh?
I was not conscious of it. It is a fashion,
A silly—a most silly fashion I have
When I am *very* happy. Did I sigh? (*sighing.*)
Aless. Thou didst. Thou art not well. Thou hast
    indulged
Too much of late, and I am vexed to see it.
Late hours and wine, Castiglione,—these
Will ruin thee! thou art already altered—
Thy looks are haggard—nothing so wears away
The constitution as late hours and wine.
Cas.(*musing.*) Nothing, fair cousin, nothing—not even
    deep sorrow—
Wears it away like evil hours and wine.
I will amend.

Aless. Do it! I would have thee drop
Thy riotous company, too—fellows low born—
Ill suit the like with old Di Broglio's heir
And Alessandra's husband.

Cas. I will drop them.

Aless. Thou wilt—thou must. Attend thou also more
To thy dress and equipage—they are over plain
For thy lofty rank and fashion—much depends
Upon appearances.

Cas. I'll see to it.

Aless. Then see to it!—pay more attention, sir,
To a becoming carriage—much thou wantest
In dignity.

Cas. Much, much, oh much I want
In proper dignity.

Aless. (*haughtily.*) Thou mockest me, sir!

Cas. (*abstractedly.*) Sweet, gentle Lalage!

Aless. Heard I aright?
I speak to him—he speaks of Lalage!
Sir Count! (*places her hand on his shoulder*) what art thou
     dreaming? he's not well!
What ails thee, sir?

Cas. (*starting.*) Cousin! fair cousin!—madam!
I crave thy pardon—indeed I am not well—
Your hand from off my shoulder, if you please.
This air is most oppressive!—Madam—the Duke!

          Enter Di Broglio.

Di Broglio. My son, I've news for thee!—hey?— what's
     the matter? (*observing Alessandra.*)
I' the pouts? Kiss her, Castiglione! kiss her,
You dog! and make it up, I say, this minute!

I've news for you both. Politian is expected
Hourly in Rome—Politian, Earl of Leicester!
We'll have him at the wedding. 'Tis his first visit
To the imperial city.

    Aless. What! Politian
Of Britain, Earl of Leicester?

    Di Brog. The same, my love.
We'll have him at the wedding. A man quite young
In years, but grey in fame. I have not seen him,
But Rumour speaks of him as of a prodigy
Pre-eminent in arts and arms, and wealth,
And high descent. We'll have him at the wedding.

    Aless. I have heard much of this Politian.
Gay, volatile and giddy—is he not?
And little given to thinking.

    Di Brog. Far from it, love.
No branch, they say, of all philosophy
So deep abstruse he has not mastered it.
Learned as few are learned.

    Aless. 'Tis very strange!
I have known men have seen Politian
And sought his company. They speak of him
As of one who entered madly into life.
Drinking the cup of pleasure to the dregs.

    Cas. Ridiculous! Now *I* have seen Politian
And know him well—nor learned nor mirthful he.
He is a dreamer and a man shut out
From common passions.

    Di Brog. Children, we disagree.
Let us go forth and taste the fragrant air

Of the garden. Did I dream, or did I hear
Politian was a *melancholy* man?   (*exeunt.*)

> ROME. A Lady's apartment, with a window open and looking into
> a garden. Lalage; in deep mourning, reading at a table on
> which lie some books and a hand mirror. In the back ground
> Jacinta (a servant maid) leans carelessly upon a chair.

Lal. Jacinta! is it thou?

Jac. (*pertly.*) Yes, Ma'am, I'm here.

Lal. I did not know, Jacinta, you were in waiting.
Sit down!—let not my presence trouble you—
Sit down!—for I am humble, most humble.

Jac. (*aside.*) 'Tis time.

> (*Jacinta seats herself in a side-long manner upon
> the chair, resting her elbows upon the back, and re-
> garding her mistress with a contemptuous look.
> Lalage continues to read.*)

Lal. "It in another climate, so he said,
Bore a bright golden flower, but not i' this soil!"

> (*pauses—turns over some leaves, and resumes.*)

"No lingering winters there, nor snow, nor shower—
But Ocean ever to refresh mankind
Breathes the shrill spirit of the western wind."
Oh, beautiful!—most beautiful!—how like
To what my fevered soul doth dream of Heaven!
O happy land! (*pauses.*) She died!—the maiden died!
O still more happy maiden who couldst die!
Jacinta!

> (*Jacinta returns no answer, and Lalage presently resumes.*)

Again!—a similar tale
Told of a beauteous dame beyond the sea!
Thus speaketh one Ferdinand in the words of the play—
"She died full young"—one Bossola answers him—
"I think not so—her infelicity
Seemed to have years too many"—Ah luckless lady!
Jacinta! (*still no answer.*)

      Here's a far sterner story
But like—oh, very like in its despair—
Of that Egyptian queen, winning so easily
A thousand hearts—losing at length her own.
She died. Thus endeth the history—and her maids
Lean over her and weep—two gentle maids
With gentle names—Eiros and Charmion!
Rainbow and Dove!——Jacinta!

  Jac. (*pettishly.*) Madam, what *is* it?

  Lal. Wilt thou, my good Jacinta, be so kind
As go down in the library and bring me
The Holy Evangelists.

  Jac. Pshaw! (*exit.*)

  Lal. If there be balm
For the wounded spirit in Gilead it is there!
Dew in the night time of my bitter trouble
Will there be found—"dew sweeter far than that
Which hangs like chains of pearl on Hermon hill."

    (*re-enter Jacinta, and throws a volume on the table.*)

  Jac. There, ma'am, 's the book. Indeed she is very
    troublesome. (*aside.*)

  Lal. (*astonished.*) What didst thou say, Jacinta? Have I
    done aught
To grieve thee or to vex thee?—I am sorry.

For thou hast served me long and ever been
Trust-worthy and respectful. (*resumes her reading.*)
    Jac. I can't believe
She has any more jewels—no—no—she gave me all.
    (*aside.*)
    Lal. What didst thou say, Jacinta? Now I bethink me
Thou hast not spoken lately of thy wedding.
How fares good Ugo?—and when is it to be?
Can I do aught?—is there no farther aid
Thou needest, Jacinta?
    Jac. Is there no *farther* aid!
That's meant for me. (*aside*) I'm sure, Madam, you need
    not
Be always throwing those jewels in my teeth.
    Lal. Jewels! Jacinta,—now indeed, Jacinta,
I thought not of the jewels.
    Jac. Oh! perhaps not!
But then I might have sworn it. After all,
There's Ugo says the ring is only paste,
For he's sure the Count Castiglione never
Would have given a real diamond to such as you;
And at the best I'm certain, Madam, you cannot
Have use for jewels *now*. But I might have sworn it.   (*exit.*)
        (*Lalage bursts into tears and leans her head upon
        the table—after a short pause raises it.*)
    Lal. Poor Lalage!—and is it come to this?
Thy servant maid!—but courage!—'tis but a viper
Whom thou hast cherished to sting thee to the soul!
        (*taking up the mirror.*)
Ha! here at least's a friend—too much a friend
In earlier days—a friend will not deceive thee.

Fair mirror and true! now tell me (for thou canst)
A tale—a pretty tale—and heed thou not
Though it be rife with woe. It answers me.
It speaks of sunken eyes, and wasted cheeks,
And Beauty long deceased—remembers me
Of Joy departed—Hope, the Seraph Hope,
Inurned and entombed!—now, in a tone
Low, sad, and solemn, but most audible,
Whispers of early grave untimely yawning
For ruined maid. Fair mirror and true!—thou liest not!
Thou hast no end to gain—no heart to break—
Castiglione lied who said he loved——
Thou true—he false!—false!—false!

> (*while she speaks, a monk enters her apartment,
> and approaches unobserved.*)

Monk, Refuge thou hast,
Sweet daughter! in Heaven. Think of eternal things!
Give up thy soul to penitence, and pray!

   Lal. (*arising hurriedly.*) I *cannot* pray!—My soul is at
      war with God!
The frightful sounds of merriment below
Disturb my senses—go! I cannot pray—
The sweet airs from the garden worry me!
Thy presence grieves me—go!—thy priestly raiment
Fills me with dread—thy ebony crucifix
With horror and awe!

   Monk. Think of thy precious soul!

   Lal. Think of my early days!—think of my father
And mother in Heaven! think of our quiet home,
And the rivulet that ran before the door!
Think of my little sisters!—think of them!

And think of me!—think of my trusting love
And confidence—his vows—my ruin—think—think
Of my unspeakable misery!——begone!
Yet stay! yet stay!—what was it thou saidst of prayer
And penitence? Didst thou not speak of faith
And vows before the throne?

    Monk. I did.

    Lal. 'Tis well.

There *is* a vow were fitting should be made—
A sacred vow, imperative, and urgent,
A solemn vow!

    Monk. Daughter, this zeal is well!

    Lal. Father, this zeal is anything but well!
Hast thou a crucifix fit for this thing?
A crucifix whereon to register
This sacred vow? (*he hands her his own.*)
Not that—Oh! no!—no!—no! (*shuddering.*)
Not that! Not that!—I tell thee, holy man,
Thy raiments and thy ebony cross affright me!
Stand back! I have a crucifix myself,—
I have a crucifix! Methinks 'twere fitting
The deed—the vow—the symbol of the deed—
And the deed's register should tally, father!

    (*draws a cross-handled dagger and raises it on high.*)
Behold the cross wherewith a vow like mine
Is written in Heaven!

    Monk. Thy words are madness, daughter,
And speak a purpose unholy—thy lips are livid—
Thine eyes are wild—tempt not the wrath divine!
Pause ere too late!—oh be not—be not rash!
Swear not the oath—oh swear it not!

    Lal. 'Tis sworn!

III

An apartment in a palace. Politian and Baldazzar.

Baldazzar.—Arouse thee now, Politian!
Thou must not—nay indeed, indeed, thou shalt not
Give way unto these humours. Be thyself!
Shake off the idle fancies that beset thee,
And live, for now thou diest!
    Politian. Not so, Baldazzar!
Surely I live.
    Bal. Politian, it doth grieve me
To see thee thus.
    Pol. Baldazzar, it doth grieve me
To give thee cause for grief, my honoured friend.
Command me, sir! what wouldst thou have me do?
At thy behest I will shake off that nature
Which from my forefathers I did inherit,
Which with my mother's milk I did imbibe,
And be no more Politian, but some other.
Command me, sir!
    Bal. To the field then—to the field—
To the senate or the field.
    Pol. Alas! alas!
There is an imp would follow me even there!
There is an imp *hath* followed me even there!
There is——what voice was that?
    Bal. I heard it not.
I heard not any voice except thine own,
And the echo of thine own.
    Pol. Then I but dreamed.
    Bal. Give not thy soul to dreams: the camp—the court

Befit thee—Fame awaits thee—Glory calls—
And her the trumpet-tongued thou wilt not hear
In hearkening to imaginary sounds
And phantom voices.

    Pol. It *is* a phantom voice!
Didst thou not hear it *then*?

    Bal. I heard it not.

    Pol. Thou heardst it not!——Baldazzar, speak no
      more
To me, Politian, of thy camps and courts.
Oh! I am sick, sick, sick, even unto death,
Of the hollow and high-sounding vanities
Of the populous Earth! Bear with me yet awhile!
We have been boys together—school-fellows—
And now are friends—yet shall not be so long—
For in the eternal city thou shalt do me
A kind and gentle office, and a Power—
A Power august, benignant and supreme—
Shall then absolve thee of all farther duties
Unto thy friend.

    Bal. Thou speakest a fearful riddle
I *will* not understand.

    Pol. Yet now as Fate
Approaches, and the Hours are breathing low,
The sands of Time are changed to golden grains,
And dazzle me, Baldazzar. Alas! alas!
I *cannot* die, having within my heart
So keen a relish for the beautiful
As hath been kindled within it. Methinks the air
Is balmier now than it was wont to be—
Rich melodies are floating in the winds—

A rarer loveliness bedecks the earth—
And with a holier lustre the quiet moon
Sitteth in Heaven.—Hist! hist! thou canst not say
Thou hearest not *now*, Baldazzar?

   Bal. Indeed I hear not.

   Pol. Not hear it!—listen now—listen!—the faintest
     sound
And yet the sweetest that ear ever heard!
A lady's voice!—and sorrow in the tone!
Baldazzar, it oppresses me like a spell!
Again!—again!—how solemnly it falls
Into my heart of hearts! that eloquent voice
Surely I never heard—yet it were well
Had I *but* heard it with its thrilling tones
In earlier days!

   Bal. I myself hear it now.
Be still!—the voice, if I mistake not greatly,
Proceeds from yonder lattice—which you may see
Very plainly through the window—it belongs,
Does it not? unto this palace of the Duke.
The singer is undoubtedly beneath
The roof of his Excellency—and perhaps
Is even that Alessandra of whom he spoke
As the betrothed of Castiglione,
His son and heir.

   Pol. Be still!—it comes again!

Voice	"And is thy heart so strong
(*very faintly.*)	As for to leave me thus
	Who hath loved thee so long
	In wealth and wo among?
	And is thy heart so strong

As for to leave me thus?
                    Say nay—say nay!"

Bal. The song is English, and I oft have heard it
In merry England—never so plaintively—
Hist! hist! it comes again!

Voice   "Is it so strong
(*more loudly.*)   As for to leave me thus
                    Who hath loved thee so long
                    In wealth and wo among?
                    And is thy heart so strong
                    As for to leave me thus?
                    Say nay—say nay!"

Bal. 'Tis hushed and all is still!

Pol. All *is not* still.

Bal. Let us go down.

Pol. Go down, Baldazzar, go!

Bal. The hour is growing late—the Duke awaits us,—
Thy presence is expected in the hall
Below. What ails thee, Earl Politian?

Voice   "Who hath loved thee so long,
(*distinctly.*)   In wealth and wo among,
                    And is thy heart so strong?
                    Say nay—say nay!"

Bal. Let us descend!—'tis time. Politian, give
These fancies to the wind. Remember, pray,
Your bearing lately savoured much of rudeness
Unto the Duke. Arouse thee! and remember!

Pol. Remember? I do. Lead on! I *do* remember. (*going.*)
Let us descend. Believe me I would give,
Freely would give the broad lands of my earldom
To look upon the face hidden by yon lattice—

"To gaze upon that veiled face, and hear
Once more that silent tongue."

   Bal. Let me beg you, sir,
Descend with me—the Duke may be offended.
Let us go down, I pray you.

          (*Voice loudly.*) *Say nay!—say nay!*

   Pol. (*aside.*) 'Tis strange!—'tis very strange—
methought the voice
Chimed in with my desires and bade me stay! (*approaching the window.*)
Sweet voice! I heed thee, and will surely stay.
Now be this Fancy, by Heaven, or be it Fate,
Still will I not descend. Baldazzar, make
Apology unto the Duke for me;
I go not down to-night.

   Bal. Your lordship's pleasure
Shall be attended to. Good night, Politian.

   Pol. Good night, my friend, good night.

IV

The gardens of a palace—Moonlight. Lalage and Politian.

   Lalage. And dost thou speak of love
To *me*, Politian?—dost thou speak of love
To Lalage?—ah wo—ah wo is me!
This mockery is most cruel—most cruel indeed!

   Politian. Weep not! oh, sob not thus!—thy bitter tears
Will madden me. Oh mourn not, Lalage—
Be comforted! I know—I know it all,
And *still* I speak of love. Look at me, brightest,
And beautiful Lalage!—turn here thine eyes!

Thou askest me if I could speak of love,
Knowing what I know, and seeing what I have seen.
Thou askest me that—and thus I answer thee—
Thus on my bended knee I answer thee. (*kneeling*.)
Sweet Lalage, *I love thee—love thee—love thee*;
Thro' good and ill—thro' weal and wo I *love thee*.
Not mother, with her first born on her knee,
Thrills with intenser love than I for thee.
Not on God's altar, in any time or clime,
Burned there a holier fire than burneth now
Within my spirit for *thee*. And do I love? (*arising*.)
Even for thy woes I love thee—even for thy woes—
Thy beauty and thy woes.

   Lal. Alas, proud Earl,
Thou dost forget thyself, remembering me!
How, in thy father's halls, among the maidens
Pure and reproachless of thy princely line,
Could the dishonoured Lalage abide?
Thy wife, and with a tainted memory—
My seared and blighted name, how would it tally
With the ancestral honours of thy house,
And with thy glory?

   Pol. Speak not to me of glory!
I hate—I loathe the name; I do abhor
The unsatisfactory and ideal thing.
Art thou not Lalage and I Politian?
Do I not love—art thou not beautiful—
What need we more? Ha! glory!—now speak not of it!
By all I hold most sacred and most solemn—
By all my wishes now—my fears hereafter—
By all I scorn on earth and hope in heaven—

There is no deed I would more glory in,
Than in thy cause to scoff at this same glory
And trample it under foot. What matters it—
What matters it, my fairest, and my best,
That we go down unhonoured and forgotten
Into the dust—so we descend together.
Descend together—and then—and then perchance——

 Lal. Why dost thou pause, Politian?

 Pol. And then perchance
Arise together, Lalage, and roam
The starry and quiet dwellings of the blest,
And still——

 Lal. Why dost thou pause, Politian?

 Pol. And still *together—together*.

 Lal. Now Earl of Leicester!
Thou *lovest* me, and in my heart of hearts
I feel thou lovest me truly.

 Pol. Oh, Lalage! (*throwing himself upon his knee.*)
And lovest thou *me*?

 Lal. Hist! hush! within the gloom
Of yonder trees methought a figure past—
A spectral figure, solemn, and slow, and noiseless—
Like the grim shadow Conscience, solemn and noiseless.
   (*walks across and returns.*)
I was mistaken—'twas but a giant bough
Stirred by the autumn wind. Politian!

 Pol. My Lalage—my love! why art thou moved?
Why dost thou turn so pale? Not Conscience' self,
Far less a shadow which thou likenest to it,
Should shake the firm spirit thus. But the night wind
Is chilly—and these melancholy boughs

Throw over all things a gloom.

 Lal. Politian!

Thou speakest to me of love. Knowest thou the land
With which all tongues are busy—a land new found—
Miraculously found by one of Genoa—
A thousand leagues within the golden west?
A fairy land of flowers, and fruit, and sunshine,
And crystal lakes, and over-arching forests,
And mountains, around whose towering summits the
  winds
Of Heaven untrammelled flow—which air to breathe
Is Happiness now, and will be Freedom hereafter
In days that are to come?

 Pol. O, wilt thou—wilt thou
Fly to that Paradise—my Lalage, wilt thou
Fly thither with me? There Care shall be forgotten,
And Sorrow shall be no more, and Eros be all.
And life shall then be mine, for I will live
For thee, and in thine eyes—and thou shalt be
No more a mourner—but the radiant Joys
Shall wait upon thee, and the angel Hope
Attend thee ever; and I will kneel to thee
And worship thee, and call thee my beloved,
My own, my beautiful, my love, my wife,
My all;—oh, wilt thou—wilt thou, Lalage,
Fly thither with me?

 Lal. A deed is to be done—
Castiglione lives!

 Pol. And he shall die! (*exit.*)

 Lal. (*after a pause.*) And—he—shall—die!——alas!
Castiglione die? Who spoke the words?

Where am I?—what was it he said?—Politian!
Thou *art* not gone—thou art not *gone*, Politian!
I *feel* thou art not gone—yet dare not look,
Lest I behold thee not; thou *couldst* not go
With those words upon thy lips—O, speak to me!
And let me hear thy voice—one word—one word,
To say thou art not gone,—one little sentence,
To say how thou dost scorn—how thou dost hate
My womanly weakness. Ha! ha! thou *art* not gone—
O speak to me! I *knew* thou wouldst not go!
I knew thou wouldst not, couldst not, *durst* not go.
Villain, thou *art* not gone—thou mockest me!
And thus I clutch thee—thus!——He is gone, he is
    gone—
Gone—gone. Where am I?——'tis well—'tis very well!
So that the blade be keen—the blow be sure,
'Tis well, 'tis *very* well—alas! alas! (*exit*.)

v

The suburbs. Politian alone.

Politian. This weakness grows upon me. I am faint,
And much I fear me ill—it will not do
To die ere I have lived!—Stay—stay thy hand,
O Azrael, yet awhile!—Prince of the Powers
Of Darkness and the Tomb, O pity me!
O pity me! let me not perish now,
In the budding of my Paradisal Hope!
Give me to live yet—yet a little while:
'Tis I who pray for life—I who so late
Demanded but to die!—what sayeth the Count?

Enter Baldazzar.

Baldazzar. That knowing no cause of quarrel or of
    feud
Between the Earl Politian and himself,
He doth decline your cartel.

Pol. What didst thou say?
What answer was it you brought me, good Baldazzar?
With what excessive fragrance the zephyr comes
Laden from yonder bowers!—a fairer day,
Or one more worthy Italy, methinks
No mortal eyes have seen!—*what* said the Count?

Bal. That he, Castiglione, not being aware
Of any feud existing, or any cause
Of quarrel between your lordship and himself
Cannot accept the challenge.

Pol. It is most true—
All this is very true. When saw you, sir,
When saw you now, Baldazzar, in the frigid
Ungenial Britain which we left so lately,
A heaven so calm as this—so utterly free
From the evil taint of clouds?—and he did *say*?

Bal. No more, my lord, than I have told you, sir:
The Count Castiglione will not fight,
Having no cause for quarrel.

Pol. Now this is true—
All very true. Thou art my friend, Baldazzar,
And I have not forgotten it—thou'lt do me
A piece of service; wilt thou go back and say
Unto this man, that I, the Earl of Leicester,
Hold him a villain?—thus much, I prythee, say
Unto the Count—it is exceeding just

He should have cause for quarrel.

    Bal. My lord!—my friend!——

    Pol. (*aside.*) 'Tis he—he comes himself! (*aloud.*) thou
       reasonest well.

I know what thou wouldst say—not send the message—
Well!—I will think of it—I will not send it.
Now prythee, leave me—hither doth come a person
With whom affairs of a most private nature
I would adjust.

    Bal. I go—to-morrow we meet,
Do we not?—at the Vatican.

    Pol. At the Vatican. (*exit Bal.*)

          Enter Castiglione.

    Cas. The Earl of Leicester here!

    Pol. I *am* the Earl of Leicester, and thou seest,
Dost thou not? that I am here.

    Cas. My lord, some strange,
Some singular mistake—misunderstanding—
Hath without doubt arisen: thou hast been urged
Thereby, in heat of anger, to address
Some words most unaccountable, in writing,
To me, Castiglione; the bearer being
Baldazzar, Duke of Surrey. I am aware
Of nothing which might warrant thee in this thing,
Having given thee no offence. Ha!—am I right?
'Twas a mistake?—undoubtedly—we all
Do err at times.

    Pol. Draw, villain, and prate no more!

    Cas. Ha!—draw?—and villain? have at thee then at
       once,
Proud Earl! (*draws.*)

Pol. (*drawing.*) Thus to the expiatory tomb,
Untimely sepulchre, I do devote thee
In the name of Lalage!

    Cas. (*letting fall his sword and recoiling to the extremity of
    the stage.*)

Of Lalage!
Hold off—thy sacred hand!—avaunt I say!
Avaunt—I will not fight thee—indeed I dare not.

    Pol. Thou wilt not fight with me didst say, Sir Count?
Shall I be baffled thus?—now this is well;
Didst say thou *darest* not? Ha!

    Cas. I dare not—dare not—
Hold off thy hand—with that beloved name
So fresh upon thy lips I will not fight thee—
I cannot—dare not.

    Pol. Now by my halidom
I do believe thee!—coward, I do believe thee!

    Cas. Ha!—coward!—this may not be!

        (*clutches his sword and staggers towards Politian,
        but his purpose is changed before reaching him, and
        he falls upon his knee at the feet of the Earl.*)

        Alas! my lord,
It is—it is—most true. In such a cause
I am the veriest coward. O pity me!

    Pol. (*greatly softened.*) Alas!—I do—indeed I pity thee.

    Cas. And Lalage——

    Pol. Scoundrel!—arise and die!

    Cas. It needeth not be—thus—thus—O let me die
Thus on my bended knee. It were most fitting
That in this deep humiliation I perish.
For in the fight I will not raise a hand

Against thee, Earl of Leicester. Strike thou home—
          (*baring his bosom.*)
Here is no let or hindrance to thy weapon—
Strike home. I *will not* fight thee.

    Pol. Now s' Death and Hell!
Am I not—am I not sorely—grievously tempted
To take thee at thy word? But mark me, sir!
Think not to fly me thus. Do thou prepare
For public insult in the streets—before
The eyes of the citizens. I'll follow thee—
Like an avenging spirit I'll follow thee
Even unto death. Before those whom thou lovest—
Before all Rome I'll taunt thee, villain,—I'll taunt thee,
Dost hear? with *cowardice*—thou *wilt not* fight me?
Thou liest! thou *shalt*! (*exit.*)

    Cas. Now this indeed is just!
Most righteous, and most just, avenging Heaven!

SELECTED PROSE

Tamerlane and Other Poems—1827

The greater part of the Poems which compose this little volume, were written in the year 1821–2, when the author had not completed his fourteenth year. They were of course not intended for publication; why they are now published concerns no one but himself. Of the smaller pieces very little need be said: they perhaps savour too much of Egotism; but they were written by one too young to have any knowledge of the world but from his own breast.

In Tamerlane, he has endeavoured to expose the folly of even *risking* the best feelings of the heart at the shrine of Ambition. He is conscious that in this there are many faults, (besides that of the general character of the poem) which he flatters himself he could, with little trouble, have corrected, but unlike many of his predecessors, has been too fond of his early productions to amend them in his *old age*.

He will not say that he is indifferent as to the success of these Poems—it might stimulate him to other attempts—but he can safely assert that failure will not at all influence him in a resolution already adopted. This is challenging criticism—let it be so. *Nos hæc novimus esse nihil.*

LETTER TO MR. —— ——

Tell wit how much it wrangles
In fickle points of niceness—
Tell wisdom it entangles
Itself in overwiseness.
        Sir Walter Raleigh

West Point, —— 1831.

Dear B——

Believing only a portion of my former volume to be worthy a second edition—that small portion I thought it as well to include in the present book as to republish by itself. I have, therefore, herein combined Al Aaraaf and Tamerlane with other Poems hitherto unprinted. Nor have I hesitated to insert from the "Minor Poems," now omitted, whole lines, and even passages, to the end that being placed in a fairer light, and the trash shaken from them in which they were imbedded, they may have some chance of being seen by posterity.

It has been said, that a good critique on a poem may be written by one who is no poet himself. This, according to *your* idea and *mine* of poetry, I feel to be false—the less poetical the critic, the less just the critique, and the converse. On this account, and because there are but few B——s in the world, I would be as much ashamed of the world's good opinion as proud of your own. Another than yourself might here observe "Shakspeare is in possession of the world's good opinion, and yet Shakspeare is the greatest of poets. It appears then that the world judge correctly, why should you be ashamed of their favorable judgment?" The difficulty lies in the interpretation of the word "judgment" or "opinion." The opinion is the world's, truly, but it may be called theirs as a man would call a book his, having bought it: he did not write the book, but it is his; they did not originate the opinion, but it is theirs. A fool, for example, thinks Shakspeare a great poet—yet the fool has never read Shakspeare. But the fool's neighbor, who is a step higher on the Andes of the mind, whose head (that is to say his more exalted thought) is too far above the fool to be seen or understood, but whose feet (by which I mean his every day actions) are sufficiently near to be discerned, and by means of which that superiority is ascertained, which *but* for them would never have been discovered—this neighbor asserts that Shakspeare is a great poet—the fool believes him, and it is henceforward his *opinion*. This neighbor's own opinion has, in like manner, been adopted from one above *him*, and so, ascendingly, to a few gifted individuals, who kneel around the summit, beholding, face to face, the master spirit who stands upon the pinnacle.

You are aware of the great barrier in the path of an American writer. He is read, if at all, in preference to the combined and established wit of the world. I say established; for it is with literature as with law or empire—an established name is an estate in tenure, or a throne in possession. Besides, one might suppose that books, like their authors, improve by travel—their having crossed the sea is, with us, so great a distinction. Our antiquaries abandon time for distance; our very fops glance from the binding to the bottom of the title-page, where the mystic characters which spell London, Paris, or Genoa, are precisely so many letters of recommendation.

I mentioned just now a vulgar error as regards criticism. I think the notion that no poet can form a correct estimate of his own writings is another. I remarked before, that in proportion to the poetical talent, would be the justice of a critique upon poetry. Therefore, a bad poet would,

I grant, make a false critique, and his self-love would infallibly bias his little judgment in his favor; but a poet, who is indeed a poet, could not, I think, fail of making a just critique. Whatever should be deducted on the score of self-love, might be replaced on account of his intimate acquaintance with the subject; in short, we have more instances of false criticism than of just, where one's own writings are the test, simply because we have more bad poets than good. There are of course many objections to what I say: Milton is a great example of the contrary; but his opinion with respect to the Paradise Regained, is by no means fairly ascertained. By what trivial circumstances men are often led to assert what they do not really believe! Perhaps an inadvertent word has descended to posterity. But, in fact, the Paradise Regained is little, if at all, inferior to the Paradise Lost, and is only supposed so to be because men do not like epics, whatever they may say to the contrary, and reading those of Milton in their natural order, are too much wearied with the first to derive any pleasure from the second.

I dare say Milton preferred Comus to either—if so—justly.

As I am speaking of poetry, it will not be amiss to touch slightly upon the most singular heresy in its modern history—the heresy of what is called very foolishly, the Lake School. Some years ago I might have been induced, by an occasion like the present, to attempt a formal refutation of their doctrine; at present it would be a work of supererogation. The wise must bow to the wisdom of such men as Coleridge and Southey, but being wise, have laughed at poetical theories so prosaically exemplified.

Aristotle, with singular assurance, has declared poetry the most philosophical of all writing*—but it required a

* Spoudiotaton kai philosophikotaton genos.

Wordsworth to pronounce it the most metaphysical. He seems to think that the end of poetry is, or should be, instruction—yet it is a truism that the end of our existence is happiness; if so, the end of every separate part of our existence—every thing connected with our existence should be still happiness. Therefore the end of instruction should be happiness; and happiness is another name for pleasure;—therefore the end of instruction should be pleasure: yet we see the above mentioned opinion implies precisely the reverse.

To proceed: ceteris paribus, he who pleases, is of more importance to his fellow men than he who instructs, since utility is happiness, and pleasure is the end already obtained which instruction is merely the means of obtaining.

I see no reason, then, why our metaphysical poets should plume themselves so much on the utility of their works, unless indeed they refer to instruction with eternity in view; in which case, sincere respect for their piety would not allow me to express my contempt for their judgment; contempt which it would be difficult to conceal, since their writings are professedly to be understood by the few, and it is the many who stand in need of salvation. In such case I should no doubt be tempted to think of the devil in Melmoth, who labors indefatigably through three octavo volumes, to accomplish the destruction of one or two souls, while any common devil would have demolished one or two thousand.

Against the subtleties which would make poetry a study—not a passion—it becomes the metaphysician to reason—but the poet to protest. Yet Wordsworth and Coleridge are men in years; the one imbued in contemplation from his childhood, the other a giant in intellect and learning. The diffidence, then, with which I venture to dispute their authority would be overwhelming, did I not feel, from the bottom of my heart, that learning has little to do with the imagination—intellect with the passions—or age with poetry.

"Trifles, like straws, upon the surface flow,
  He who would search for pearls must dive below,"

are lines which have done much mischief. As regards the greater truths, men oftener err by seeking them at the bottom than at the top; the depth lies in the huge abysses where wisdom is sought—not in the palpable palaces where she is found. The ancients were not always right in hiding the goddess in a well: witness the light which Bacon has thrown upon philosophy; witness the principles of our divine faith—that moral mechanism by which the simplicity of a child may overbalance the wisdom of a man.

Poetry, above all things, is a beautiful painting whose tints, to minute inspection, are confusion worse confounded, but start boldly out to the cursory glance of the connoisseur.

We see an instance of Coleridge's liability to err in his Biographia Litteraria—professedly his literary life and opinions, but, in fact, a treatise *de omni scibili et quibusdam aliis*. He goes wrong by reason of his very profundity, and of his error we have a natural type in the contemplation of a star. He who regards it directly and intensely sees, it is true, the star, but it is the star without a ray—while he who surveys it less inquisitively is conscious of all for which the star is useful to us below—its brilliancy and its beauty.

As to Wordsworth, I have no faith in him: That he had, in youth, the feelings of a poet, I believe—for there are glimpses of extreme delicacy in his writings—(and delicacy is the poet's own kingdom—his *El Dorado*)—but they have the appearance of a better day recollected; and glimpses, at best, are little evidence of present poetic fire—we know that a few straggling flowers spring up daily in the crevices of the Avalanche.

He was to blame in wearing away his youth in contemplation with the end of poetizing in his manhood. With the increase of his judgment the light which should make it apparent has faded away. His judgment consequently is too correct. This may not be understood, but the old Goths of Germany would have understood it, who used to debate matters of importance to their State twice, once when drunk, and once when sober—sober that they might not be deficient in formality—drunk lest they should be destitute of vigor.

The long wordy discussions by which he tries to reason us into admiration of his poetry, speak very little in his favor: they are full of such assertions as this—(I have opened one of his volumes at random) "Of genius the only proof is the act of doing well what is worthy to be done, and what was never done before"—indeed: then it follows that in doing what is *un*worthy to be done, or what *has* been done before, no genius can be evinced: yet the picking of pockets is an unworthy act, pockets have been picked time immemorial, and Barrington, the pick-pocket, in point of genius, would have thought hard of a comparison with William Wordsworth, the poet.

Again—in estimating the merit of certain poems, whether they be Ossian's or M'Pherson's, can surely be of little consequence, yet, in order to prove their worthlessness, Mr. W. has expended many pages in the controversy. *Tantæne animis?* Can great minds descend to such absurdity? But worse still: that he may bear down every argument in favor of these poems, he triumphantly drags forward a passage in his abomination of which he expects the reader to sympathize. It is the beginning of the epic poem "*Temora*." "The blue waves of Ullin roll in light; the green hills are covered with day; trees shake their dusky heads in the breeze." And this—this gorgeous, yet simple imagery—where all is alive and panting with immortality—than which earth has nothing more grand, nor paradise more beautiful—this—William Wordsworth, the author of Peter Bell, has *selected* to dignify with his imperial contempt. We shall see what better he, in his own person, has to offer. Imprimis:

> "And now she's at the poney's head,
> And now she's at the poney's tail,
> On that side now, and now on this,
> And almost stifled her with bliss—
> A few sad tears does Betty shed,
> She pats the poney where or when
> She knows not: happy Betty Foy!
> O Johnny! never mind the Doctor!"

Secondly:

"The dew was falling fast, the—stars began to blink,
I heard a voice, it said——drink, pretty creature, drink;
And looking o'er the hedge, be—fore me I espied
A snow-white mountain lamb with a—maiden at its side.
No other sheep were near, the lamb was all alone.
And by a slender cord was—tether'd to a stone."

Now we have no doubt this is all true; we *will* believe it, indeed we will, Mr. W. Is it sympathy for the sheep you wish to excite? I love a sheep from the bottom of my heart.

But there *are* occasions, dear B——, there are occasions when even Wordsworth is reasonable. Even Stamboul, it is said, shall have an end, and the most unlucky blunders must come to a conclusion. Here is an extract from his preface.

"Those who have been accustomed to the phrase-ology of modern writers, if they persist in reading this book to a conclusion (*impossible!*) will, no doubt, have to struggle with feelings of awkwardness; (ha! ha! ha!) they will look round for poetry (ha! ha! ha! ha!) and will be induced to inquire by what species of courtesy these attempts have been permitted to assume that title." Ha! ha! ha! ha! ha!

Yet let not Mr. W. despair; he has given immortality to a wagon, and the bee Sophocles has eternalized a sore toe, and dignified a tragedy with a chorus of turkeys.

Of Coleridge I cannot speak but with reverence. His towering intellect! his gigantic power! To use an author quoted by himself, "Jai trouve souvent que la plupart des sectes ont raison dans une bonne partie de ce quelles avancent, mais non pas en ce quelles nient," and, to employ his own language, he has imprisoned his own conceptions by the barrier he has erected against those of others. It is lamentable to think that such a mind should be buried in metaphysics, and, like the Nyctanthes, waste its perfume upon the night alone. In reading that man's poetry I tremble, like one who stands upon a volcano, conscious, from the very darkness bursting from the crater, of the fire and the light that are weltering below.

What is Poetry? Poetry! that Proteus-like idea, with as many appellations as the nine-titled Corcyra! Give me, I demanded of a scholar some time ago, give me a definition of poetry? "Tres volontiers,"—and he proceeded to his library, brought me a Dr. Johnson, and overwhelmed me with a definition. Shade of the immortal Shakspeare! I imagined to myself the scowl of your spiritual eye upon the profanity of that scurrilous Ursa Major. Think of poetry, dear B——, think of poetry, and then think of—Dr. Samuel Johnson! Think of all that is airy and fairy-like, and then of all that is hideous and unwieldy; think of his huge bulk, the Elephant! and then—and then think of the Tempest—the Midsummer Night's Dream—Prospero—Oberon—and Titania!

A poem, in my opinion, is opposed to a work of science by having, for its *immediate* object, pleasure, not truth; to romance, by having for its object an *indefinite* instead of a *definite* pleasure, being a poem only so far as this object is attained: romance presenting perceptible images with definite, poetry with *in*definite sensations, to which end music is an *essential*, since the comprehension of sweet sound is our most indefinite conception. Music, when combined with a pleasurable idea, is poetry; music without the idea is simply music; the idea without the music is prose from its very definitiveness.

What was meant by the invective against "him who had no music in his soul?"

To sum up this long rigmarole, I have, dear B——, what you no doubt perceive, for the metaphysical poets, *as* poets, the most sovereign contempt. That they have followers proves nothing—

> No Indian prince has to his palace
> More followers than a thief to the gallows.

The Raven and Other Poems—1845

These trifles are collected and republished chiefly with a view to their redemption from the many improvements to which they have been subjected while going at random "the rounds of the press." If what I have written is to circulate at all, I am naturally anxious that it should circulate as I wrote it. In defence of my own taste, nevertheless, it is incumbent upon me to say, that I think nothing in this volume of much value to the public, or very creditable to myself. Events not to be controlled have prevented me from making, at any time, any serious effort in what, under happier circumstances, would have been the field of my choice. With me poetry has been not a purpose, but a passion; and the passions should be held in reverence; they must not—they cannot at will be excited with an eye to the paltry compensations, or the more paltry commendations, of mankind.

FROM
The Poetic Principle

While the epic mania—while the idea that, to merit in poetry, prolixity is indispensable—has, for some years past, been gradually dying out of the public mind, by mere dint of its own absurdity—we find it succeeded by a heresy too palpably false to be long tolerated, but one which, in the brief period it has already endured, may be said to have accomplished more in the corruption of our Poetical Literature than all its other enemies combined. I allude to the heresy of *The Didactic*. It has been assumed, tacitly and avowedly, directly and indirectly, that the ultimate object of all Poetry is Truth. Every poem, it is said, should inculcate a moral; and by this moral is the poetical merit of the work to be adjudged. We Americans, especially, have patronised this happy idea; and we Bostonians, very especially, have developed it in full. We have taken it into our heads that to write a poem simply for the poem's sake, and to acknowledge such to have been our design, would be to confess ourselves radically wanting in the true Poetic dignity and force:—but the simple fact is, that, would we but permit ourselves to look into our own souls, we should immediately there discover that under the sun there neither exists nor *can* exist any work more thoroughly dignified—more supremely noble than this very poem—this poem *per se*—this poem which is a poem and nothing more—this poem written solely for the poem's sake.

With as deep a reverence for the True as ever inspired the bosom of man, I would, nevertheless, limit, in some measure, its modes of inculcation. I would limit to enforce them. I would not enfeeble them by dissipation. The demands of Truth are severe. She has no sympathy with the myrtles. All *that* which is so indispensable in Song, is precisely all *that* with which *she* has nothing whatever to do. It is but making her a flaunting paradox, to wreathe her in gems and flowers. In enforcing a truth, we need severity rather than efflorescence of language. We must be simple, precise, terse. We must be cool, calm, unimpassioned. In a word, we must be in that mood which, as nearly as possible, is the exact converse of the poetical. *He* must be blind, indeed, who does not perceive the radical and chasmal differences between the truthful and the poetical modes of inculcation. He must be theory-mad beyond redemption who, in spite of these differences, shall still persist in attempting to reconcile the obstinate oils and waters of Poetry and Truth.

Dividing the world of mind into its three most immediately obvious distinctions, we have the Pure Intellect, Taste, and the Moral Sense. I place Taste in the middle, because it is just this position, which, in the mind, it occupies. It holds intimate relations with either extreme; but from the Moral Sense is separated by so faint a difference that Aristotle has not hesitated to place some of its operations among the virtues themselves. Nevertheless, we find the *offices* of the trio marked with a sufficient distinction. Just as the Intellect concerns itself with Truth, so Taste informs us of the Beautiful while the Moral Sense is regardful of Duty. Of this latter, while Conscience teaches the obligation, and Reason the expediency, Taste contents herself with displaying the charms:—waging war upon Vice solely on the ground of her deformity—her disproportion—her animosity to the fitting, to the appropriate, to the harmonious—in a word, to Beauty.

An immortal instinct, deep within the spirit of man, is

thus, plainly, a sense of the Beautiful. This it is which administers to his delight in the manifold forms, and sounds, and odours, and sentiments amid which he exists. And just as the lily is repeated in the lake, or the eyes of Amaryllis in the mirror, so is the mere oral or written repetition of these forms, and sounds, and colours, and odours, and sentiments, a duplicate source of delight. But this mere repetition is not poetry. He who shall simply sing, with however glowing enthusiasm, or with however vivid a truth of description, of the sights, and sounds, and odours, and colours, and sentiments, which greet *him* in common with all mankind—he, I say, has yet failed to prove his divine title. There is still a something in the distance which he has been unable to attain. We have still a thirst unquenchable, to allay which he has not shown us the crystal springs. This thirst belongs to the immortality of Man. It is at once a consequence and an indication of his perennial existence. It is the desire of the moth for the star. It is no mere appreciation of the Beauty before us—but a wild effort to reach the Beauty above. Inspired by an ecstatic prescience of the glories beyond the grave, we struggle, by multiform combinations among the things and thoughts of Time, to attain a portion of that Loveliness whose very elements, perhaps, appertain to eternity alone. And thus when by Poetry—or when by Music, the most entrancing of the Poetic moods—we find ourselves melted into tears— we weep then—not as the Abbaté Gravina supposes— through excess of pleasure, but through a certain, petulant, impatient sorrow at our inability to grasp *now*, wholly, here on earth, at once and for ever, those divine and rapturous joys, of which *through* the poem, or *through* the music, we attain to but brief and indeterminate glimpses.

The struggle to apprehend the supernal Loveliness—

this struggle, on the part of souls fittingly constituted—has given to the world all *that* which it (the world) has ever been enabled at once to understand and *to feel* as poetic.

The Poetic Sentiment, of course, may develope itself in various modes—in Painting, in Sculpture, in Architecture, in the Dance—very especially in Music—and very peculiarly, and with a wide field, in the composition of the Landscape Garden. Our present theme, however, has regard only to its manifestation in words. And here let me speak briefly on the topic of rhythm. Contenting myself with the certainty that Music, in its various modes of metre, rhythm, and rhyme, is of so vast a moment in Poetry as never to be wisely rejected—is so vitally important an adjunct, that he is simply silly who declines its assistance, I will not now pause to maintain its absolute essentiality. It is in Music, perhaps, that the soul most nearly attains the great end for which, when inspired with the Poetic Sentiment, it struggles—the creation of supernal Beauty. It *may* be, indeed, that here this sublime end is, now and then, attained *in fact*. We are often made to feel, with a shivering delight, that from an earthly harp are stricken notes which *cannot* have been unfamiliar to the angels. And thus there can be little doubt that in the union of Poetry with Music in its popular sense, we shall find the widest field for the Poetic development. The old Bards and Minnesingers had advantages which we do not possess—and Thomas Moore, singing his own songs, was, in the most legitimate manner, perfecting them as poems.

To recapitulate, then:—I would define, in brief, the Poetry of words as *The Rhythmical Creation of Beauty*. Its sole arbiter is Taste. With the Intellect or with the Conscience, it has only collateral relations. Unless incidentally, it has no concern whatever either with Duty or with Truth.

A few words, however, in explanation. *That* pleasure which is at once the most pure, the most elevating, and the most intense, is derived, I maintain, from the contemplation of the Beautiful. In the contemplation of Beauty we alone find it possible to attain that pleasurable elevation, or excitement, *of the soul*, which we recognise as the Poetic Sentiment, and which is so easily distinguished from Truth, which is the satisfaction of the Reason, or from Passion, which is the excitement of the heart. I make Beauty, therefore—using the word as inclusive of the sublime—I make Beauty the province of the poem, simply because it is an obvious rule of Art that effects should be made to spring as directly as possible from their causes:—no one as yet having been weak enough to deny that the peculiar elevation in question is at least *most readily* attainable in the poem. It by no means follows, however, that the incitements of Passion, or the precepts of Duty, or even the lessons of Truth, may not be introduced into a poem, and with advantage; for they may subserve, incidentally, in various ways, the general purposes of the work:—but the true artist will always contrive to tone them down in proper subjection to that *Beauty* which is the atmosphere and the real essence of the poem.

* * *

Thus, although in a very cursory and imperfect manner, I have endeavoured to convey to you my conception of the Poetic Principle. It has been my purpose to suggest that, while this Principle itself is, strictly and simply, the Human Aspiration for Supernal Beauty, the manifestation of the Principle is always found in *an elevating excitement of the Soul*—quite independent of that passion which is the intoxication of the Heart—or of that Truth which is the satisfaction of the Reason. For, in regard to Passion, alas!

its tendency is to degrade, rather than to elevate the Soul. Love, on the contrary—Love—the true, the divine Eros— the Uranian, as distinguished from the Dionæan Venus— is unquestionably the purest and truest of all poetical themes. And in regard to Truth—if, to be sure, through the attainment of a truth, we are led to perceive a harmony where none was apparent before, we experience, at once, the true poetical effect—but this effect is referable to the harmony alone, and not in the least degree to the truth which merely served to render the harmony manifest.

FROM

Review of *Orion*, by R. H. Horne

But the question is not even this. It is not whether it be not possible to introduce didacticism, with effect, into a poem, or possible to introduce poetical images and measures, with effect, into a didactic essay. To do either the one or the other, would be merely to surmount a difficulty— would be simply a feat of literary sleight of hand. But the true question is, whether the author who shall attempt either feat, will not be laboring at a disadvantage—will not be guilty of a fruitless and wasteful expenditure of energy. In minor poetical efforts, we may not so imperatively demand an adherence to the true poetical thesis. We permit *trifling* to some extent, in a work which we consider a trifle at best. Although we agree, for example, with Coleridge, that poetry and *passion* are discordant, yet we are willing to permit Tennyson to bring, to the intense *passion* which prompted his "Locksley Hall," the aid of that terseness and pungency which are derivable from rhythm and from rhyme. The effect he produces, however, is a purely passionate, and not, unless in detached passages of this magnificent philippic, a properly poetic effect. His "Œnone," on the other hand, exalts the soul not into passion, but into a conception of pure *beauty*, which in its elevation—its calm and intense rapture—has in it a foreshadowing of the future and spiritual life, and as far transcends earthly passion as the holy radiance of the sun does the glimmering and feeble phosphorescence of the glow-worm. His "Morte D'Arthur" is in the same majestic vein. The "Sensitive Plant" of Shelley is in the same sublime spirit. Nor, if the passionate poems of Byron excite more intensely a greater number of readers than either the "Œnone" or the "Sensitive Plant"—does this indisputable fact prove any thing more than that the majority of mankind are more susceptible of the impulses of passion than of the impressions of beauty. Readers do exist, however, and always will exist, who, to hearts of maddening fervor, unite, in perfection, the sentiment of the beautiful—that divine sixth sense which is yet so faintly understood—that sense which phrenology has attempted to embody in its organ of *ideality*—that sense which is the basis of all Fourier's dreams—that sense which speaks of GOD through his purest, if not his *sole* attribute—which proves, and which alone proves his existence.

To readers such as these—and only to such as these—must be left the decision of what the true Poesy is. And these—with *no* hesitation—will decide that the origin of Poetry lies in a thirst for a wilder Beauty than Earth supplies—that Poetry itself is the imperfect effort to quench this immortal thirst by novel combinations of beautiful forms (collocations of forms) physical or spiritual, and that this thirst when even partially allayed—this sentiment when even feebly meeting response—produces emotion to which all other human emotions are vapid and insignificant.

We shall now be fully understood. If, with Coleridge, who, however erring at times, was precisely the mind fitted to decide a question such as this—if, with him, we reject *passion* from the true—from the pure poetry—if we reject even passion—if we discard as feeble, as unworthy the high spirituality of the theme, (which has its origin in a sense of the Godhead) if we dismiss even the nearly divine emotion of human *love*—that emotion which, merely to name, *now* causes the pen to tremble—with how much greater reason shall we dismiss all else? And yet there are men who would mingle with the august theme the merest questions of expediency—the cant topics of the day—the doggerel æsthetics of the time—who would trammel the soul in its flight to an ideal Helusion, by the quirks and quibbles of chopped logic. There are men who do this— lately there are a set of men who make a practice of doing this—and who defend it on the score of the advancement of what they suppose to be *truth*. Truth is, in its own essence, sublime—but her loftiest sublimity, as derived from man's clouded and erratic reason, is valueless—is pulseless—is utterly ineffective when brought into comparison with the unerring *sense* of which we speak; yet grant this *truth* to be all which its seekers and worshipers pretend—they forget that it is not truth, *per se*, which is made their thesis, but an *argumentation*, often maudlin and pedantic, always shallow and unsatisfactory (as from the mere inadaptation of the vehicle it *must* be) by which this *truth*, in casual and indeterminate glimpses, is—*or is not*— rendered manifest.

Review of *Alciphron*, by Thomas Moore

The truth is that the just distinction between the fancy and the imagination (and which is still but a distinction *of degree*) is involved in the consideration of the *mystic*. We give this as an idea of our own, altogether. We have no authority for our opinion—but do not the less firmly hold it. The term *mystic* is here employed in the sense of Augustus William Schlegel, and of most other German critics. It is applied by them to that class of composition in which there lies beneath the transparent upper current of meaning, an under or *suggestive* one. What we vaguely term the *moral* of any sentiment is its mystic or secondary expression. It has the vast force of an accompaniment in music. This vivifies the air; that spiritualizes the *fanciful* conception, and lifts it into the *ideal*.

This theory will bear, we think, the most rigorous tests which can be made applicable to it, and will be acknowledged as tenable by all who are themselves imaginative. If we carefully examine those poems, or portions of poems, or those prose romances, which mankind have been accustomed to designate as *imaginative*, (for an instinctive feeling leads us to employ properly the term whose full import we have still never been able to define,) it will be seen that all so designated are remarkable for the *suggestive* character which we have discussed. They are strongly *mystic*—in the proper sense of the word. We will here only call to the reader's mind, the *Prometheus Vinctus* of Æschylus; the *Inferno* of Dante; the *Destruction of Numantia* by Cervantes; the *Comus* of Milton; the *Auncient Mariner*, the *Christabel*, and the *Kubla Khan*, of Coleridge; the *Nightingale* of Keats; and, most especially, the *Sensitive*

Plant of Shelley, and the *Undine* of De La Motte Fouqué. These two latter poems (for we call them both such) are the finest possible examples of the purely *ideal*. There is little of fancy here, and every thing of imagination. With each note of the lyre is heard a ghostly, and not always a distinct, but an august and soul-exalting *echo*. In every glimpse of beauty presented, we catch, through long and wild vistas, dim bewildering visions of a far more ethereal beauty *beyond*. But not so in poems which the world has always persisted in terming *fanciful*. Here the upper current is often exceedingly brilliant and beautiful; but then men *feel* that this upper current *is all*. No Naiad voice addresses them *from below*. The notes of the air of the song do not tremble with the according tones of the accompaniment.

FROM
A Chapter of Suggestions

That the imagination has not been unjustly ranked as supreme among the mental faculties, appears, from the intense consciousness, on the part of the imaginative man, that the faculty in question brings his soul often to a glimpse of things supernal and eternal—to the very verge of the *great secrets*. There are moments, indeed, in which he perceives the faint perfumes, and hears the melodies of a happier world. Some of the most profound knowledge —perhaps all *very* profound knowledge—has originated from a highly stimulated imagination. Great intellects *guess* well. The laws of Kepler were, professedly, *guesses*.

Marginalia

I am not sure that Tennyson is not the greatest of poets. The uncertainty attending the public conception of the term "poet" alone prevents me from demonstrating that he *is*. Other bards produce effects which are, now and then, otherwise produced than by what we call poems; but Tennyson an effect which only a poem does. His alone are idiosyncratic poems. By the enjoyment or non-enjoyment of the "Morte D'Arthur," or of the "Œnone," I would test any one's ideal sense.

There are passages in his works which rivet a conviction I had long entertained, that the *indefinite* is an element in the true ποιησις. Why do some persons fatigue themselves in attempts to unravel such phantasy-pieces as the "Lady of Shalott?" As well unweave the "*ventum textilem.*" If the author did not deliberately propose to himself a suggestive indefinitiveness of meaning, with the view of bringing about a definitiveness of vague and therefore of spiritual *effect*—this, at least, arose from the silent analytical promptings of that poetic genius which, in its supreme development, embodies all orders of intellectual capacity.

I *know* that indefinitiveness is an element of the true music—I mean of the true musical expression. Give to it any undue decision—imbue it with any very determinate tone—and you deprive it, at once, of its ethereal, its ideal, its intrinsic and essential character. You dispel its luxury of dream. You dissolve the atmosphere of the mystic upon which it floats. You exhaust it of its breath of faery. It now becomes a tangible and easy appreciable idea—a thing of the earth, earthy. It has not, indeed, lost its power to please, but all which I consider the distinctiveness of that power. And to the uncultivated talent, or to the unimaginative apprehension, this deprivation of its most delicate grace will be, not unfrequently, a recommendation. A determinateness of expression is sought—and often by composers who should know better—is sought as a beauty rather than rejected as a blemish. Thus we have, even from high authorities, attempts at absolute *imitation* in music. Who can forget the sillinesses of the "Battle of Prague?" What man of taste but must laugh at the interminable drums, trumpets, blunderbusses, and thunder? "*Vocal* music," says L'Abbate Gravina, who would have said the same thing of instrumental, "ought to imitate the natural language of the human feelings and passions, rather than the warblings of Canary birds, which our singers, now-a-days, affect so vastly to mimic with their quaverings and boasted cadences." This is true only so far as the "rather" is concerned. If any music must imitate anything, it were assuredly better to limit the imitation as Gravina suggests.

Tennyson's shorter pieces abound in minute rhythmical lapses sufficient to assure me that—in common with all poets living or dead—he has neglected to make precise investigation of the principles of metre; but, on the other hand, so perfect is his rhythmical instinct in general, that, like the present Viscount Canterbury, he seems *to see with his ear*.

———

Some Frenchman—possibly Montaigne—says: "People talk about thinking, but for my part I never think, except when I sit down to write." It is this never thinking, unless when we sit down to write, which is the cause of so much indifferent composition. But perhaps there is something more involved in the Frenchman's observation than meets the eye. It is certain that the mere act of inditing, tends, in a great degree, to the logicalization of thought. Whenever, on account of its vagueness, I am dissatisfied with a conception of the brain, I resort forthwith to the pen, for the purpose of obtaining, through its aid, the necessary form, consequence and precision.

How very commonly we hear it remarked, that such and such thoughts are beyond the compass of words! I do not believe that any thought, properly so called, is out of the reach of language. I fancy, rather, that where difficulty in expression is experienced, there is, in the intellect which experiences it, a want either of deliberateness or of method. For my own part, I have never had a thought which I could not set down in words, with even more distinctness than that with which I conceived it:—as I have before observed, the thought is logicalized by the effort at (written) expression.

There is, however, a class of fancies, of exquisite delicacy, which are *not* thoughts, and to which, *as yet*, I have found it absolutely impossible to adapt language. I use the word *fancies* at random, and merely because I must use *some* word; but the idea commonly attached to the term is not even remotely applicable to the shadows of shadows in question. They seem to me rather psychal than intellectual. They arise in the soul (alas, how rarely!) only at its epochs of most intense tranquillity—when the bodily and mental health are in perfection—and at those mere points of time where the confines of the waking world blend with those of the world of dreams. I am aware of these "fancies" only when I am upon the very brink of sleep, with the consciousness that I am so. I have satisfied myself that this condition exists but for an inappreciable *point* of time—yet it is crowded with these "shadows of shadows;" and for absolute *thought* there is demanded time's *endurance*.

These "fancies" have in them a pleasurable ecstasy as

far beyond the most pleasurable of the world of wakeful-
ness, or of dreams, as the Heaven of the Northman theol-
ogy is beyond its Hell. I regard the visions, even as they
arise, with an awe which, in some measure, moderates or
tranquilizes the ecstasy—I so regard them, through a con-
viction (which seems a portion of the ecstasy itself) that
this ecstasy, in itself, is of a character supernal to the Hu-
man Nature—is a glimpse of the spirit's outer world; and I
arrive at this conclusion—if this term is at all applicable to
instantaneous intuition—by a perception that the delight
experienced has, as its element, but *the absoluteness of
novelty*. I say the absoluteness—for in these fancies—let
me now term them psychal impressions—there is really
nothing even approximate in character to impressions or-
dinarily received. It is as if the five senses were supplanted
by five myriad others alien to mortality.

Now, so entire is my faith in the *power of words*, that,
at times, I have believed it possible to embody even the
evanescence of fancies such as I have attempted to describe.
In experiments with this end in view, I have proceeded so far
as first, to control (when the bodily and mental health are
good) the existence of the condition:—that is to say, I can
now (unless when ill) be sure that the condition will super-
vene, if I so wish it, at the point of time already described:
—of its supervention, until lately, I could never be certain,
even under the most favorable circumstances. I mean to say,
merely, that now I can be sure, when all circumstances are
favorable, of the supervention of the condition, and feel
even the capacity of inducing or compelling it:—the favor-
able circumstances, however, are not the less rare—else had
I compelled, already, the Heaven into the Earth.

I have proceeded so far, secondly, as to prevent the
lapse from *the point* of which I speak—the point of blend-
ing between wakefulness and sleep—as to prevent at will, I

say, the lapse from this border-ground into the dominion of sleep. Not that I can *continue* the condition—not that I can render the point more than a point—but that I can startle myself from the point into wakefulness—*and thus transfer the point itself into the realm of Memory*—convey its impressions, or more properly their recollections, to a situation where (although still for a very brief period) I can survey them with the eye of analysis.

For these reasons—that is to say, because I have been enabled to accomplish thus much—I do not altogether despair of embodying in words at least enough of the fancies in question to convey, to certain classes of intellect, a shadowy conception of their character.

In saying this I am not to be understood as supposing that the fancies, or psychal impressions, to which I allude, are confined to my individual self—are not, in a word, common to all mankind—for on this point it is quite impossible that I should form an opinion—but nothing can be more certain than that even a partial record of the impressions would startle the universal intellect of mankind, by the *supremeness of the novelty* of the material employed, and of its consequent suggestions. In a word—should I ever write a paper on this topic, the world will be compelled to acknowledge that, at last, I have done an original thing.

———

The *pure Imagination* chooses, from *either Beauty or Deformity*, only the most combinable things hitherto uncombined; the compound, as a general rule, partaking, in character, of beauty, or sublimity, in the ratio of the respective beauty or sublimity of the things combined—which are themselves still to be considered as atomic—that is to say, as previous combinations. But, as often analogously happens in physical chemistry, so not unfrequently does it occur in this chemistry of the intellect, that the admixture of two elements results in a something that has nothing of the qualities of one of them, or even nothing of the qualities of either . . . Thus, the range of Imagination is unlimited. Its materials extend throughout the universe. Even out of deformities it fabricates that *Beauty* which is at once its sole object and its inevitable test. But, in general, the richness or force of the matters combined; the facility of discovering combinable novelties worth combining; and, especially the absolute "chemical combination" of the completed mass—are the particulars to be regarded in our estimate of Imagination. It is this thorough harmony of an imaginative work which so often causes it to be undervalued by the thoughtless, through the character of *obviousness* which is superinduced. We are apt to find ourselves asking *why* it is that these combinations have never been imagined before.

EUREKA: A PROSE POEM

That the stellar bodies would finally be merged in one—that, at last, all would be drawn into the substance of *one stupendous central orb already existing*—is an idea which, for some time past, seems, vaguely and indeterminately, to have held possession of the fancy of mankind. It is an idea, in fact, which belongs to the class of the *excessively obvious*. It springs, instantly, from a superficial observation of the cyclic and seemingly *gyrating*, or *vorticial* movements of those individual portions of the Universe which come most immediately and most closely under our observation. There is not, perhaps, a human being, of ordinary education and of average reflective capacity, to whom, at some period, the fancy in question has not occurred, as if spontaneously, or intuitively, and wearing all the character of a very profound and very original conception. This conception, however, so commonly entertained, has never, within my knowledge, arisen out of any abstract considerations. Being, on the contrary, always suggested, as I say, by the vorticial movements about centres, a reason for it, also, —a *cause* for the ingathering of all the orbs into one, *imagined to be already existing*, was naturally sought in the same direction—among these cyclic movements themselves.

Thus it happened that, on announcement of the gradual and perfectly regular decrease observed in the orbit of Encke's comet, at every successive revolution about our Sun, astronomers were nearly unanimous in the opinion that the cause in question was found—that a principle was discovered sufficient to account, physically, for that final, universal agglomeration which, I repeat, the analogical, symmetrical or poetical instinct of Man had predetermined to understand as something more than a simple hypothesis.

This cause—this sufficient reason for the final ingathering—was declared to exist in an exceedingly rare but still material medium pervading space; which medium, by retarding, in some degree, the progress of the comet, perpetually weakened its tangential force; thus giving a predominance to the centripetal; which, of course, drew the comet nearer and nearer at each revolution, and would eventually precipitate it upon the Sun.

All this was strictly logical—admitting the medium or ether; but this ether was assumed, most illogically, on the ground that no *other* mode than the one mentioned could be discovered, of accounting for the observed decrease in the orbit of the comet:—as if from the fact that we could *discover* no other mode of accounting for it, it followed, in any respect, that no other mode of accounting for it existed. It is clear that innumerable causes might operate, in combination, to diminish the orbit, without even a possibility of our ever becoming acquainted with even one of them. In the meantime, it has never been fairly shown, perhaps, why the retardation occasioned by the skirts of the Sun's atmosphere, through which the comet passes at perihelion, is not enough to account for the phænomenon. That Encke's comet will be absorbed into the Sun, is probable; that all the comets of the system will be absorbed, is more than merely possible; but, in such case, the principle of absorption must be referred to eccentricity of orbit—to the close approximation to the Sun, of the comets at their perihelia; and is a principle not affecting, in any degree, the ponderous *spheres*, which are to be regarded as the true material constituents of the Universe.—Touching comets, in general, let me here suggest, in passing, that we cannot be far wrong in looking upon them as the *lightning-flashes of the cosmical Heaven.*

The idea of retarding ether and, through it, of a final agglomeration of all things, seemed at one time, however, to be confirmed by the observation of a positive decrease in the orbit of the solid moon. By reference to eclipses recorded 2500 years ago, it was found that the velocity of the satellite's revolution *then* was considerably less than it is *now*; that on the hypothesis that its motion in its orbit is uniformly in accordance with Kepler's law, and was accurately determined *then*—2500 years ago—it is now in advance of the position it *should* occupy, by nearly 9000 miles. The increase of velocity proved, of course, a diminution of orbit; and astronomers were fast yielding to a belief in an ether, as the sole mode of accounting for the phænomenon, when Lagrange came to the rescue. He showed that, owing to the configurations of the spheroids, the shorter axes of their ellipses are subject to variation in length; the longer axes being permanent; and that this variation is continuous and vibratory—so that every orbit is in a state of transition, either from circle to ellipse, or from ellipse to circle. In the case of the moon, where the shorter axis is *de*creasing, the orbit is passing from circle to ellipse and, consequently, is *de*creasing too; but, after a long series of ages, the ultimate eccentricity will be attained; then the shorter axis will proceed to *in*crease, until the orbit becomes a circle; when the process of shortening will again take place;—and so on forever. In the case of the Earth, the orbit is passing from ellipse to circle. The facts thus demonstrated do away, of course, with all necessity for supposing an ether, and with all apprehension of the system's instability—*on the ether's account.*

It will be remembered that I have myself assumed what we may term *an ether*. I have spoken of a subtle *in-*

fluence which we know to be ever in attendance on matter, although becoming manifest only through matter's heterogeneity. To this *influence*—without daring to touch it at all in any effort at explaining its awful *nature*—I have referred the various phænomena of electricity, heat, light, magnetism; and more—of vitality, consciousness, and thought—in a word, of spirituality. It will be seen, at once, then, that the ether thus conceived is radically distinct from the ether of the astronomers; inasmuch as theirs is *matter* and mine *not*.

With the idea of a material ether, seems, thus, to have departed altogether the thought of that universal agglomeration so long predetermined by the poetical fancy of mankind:—an agglomeration in which a sound Philosophy might have been warranted in putting faith, at least to a certain extent, if for no other reason than that by this poetical fancy it *had* been so predetermined. But so far as Astronomy—so far as mere Physics have yet spoken, the cycles of the Universe are perpetual—the Universe has no conceivable end. Had an end been demonstrated, however, from so purely collateral a cause as an ether, Man's instinct of the Divine *capacity to adapt*, would have rebelled against the demonstration. We should have been forced to regard the Universe with some such sense of dissatisfaction as we experience in contemplating an unnecessarily complex work of human art. Creation would have affected us as an imperfect *plot* in a romance, where the *dénoûment* is awkwardly brought about by interposed incidents external and foreign to the main subject; instead of springing out of the bosom of the thesis—out of the heart of the ruling idea—instead of arising as a result of the primary proposition—as inseparable and inevitable part and parcel of the fundamental conception of the book.

What I mean by the symmetry of mere surface will now be more clearly understood. It is simply by the blandishment of this symmetry that we have been beguiled into the general idea of which Mädler's hypothesis is but a part—the idea of the vorticial indrawing of the orbs. Dismissing this nakedly physical conception, the symmetry of *principle* sees the end of all things metaphysically involved in the thought of a beginning; seeks and finds, in this origin of all things, the *rudiment* of this end; and perceives the impiety of supposing this end likely to be brought about less simply—less directly—less obviously—less artistically—than through *the rëaction of the originating Act.*

Recurring, then, to a previous suggestion, let us understand the systems—let us understand each star, with its attendant planets—as but a Titanic atom existing in space with precisely the same inclination for Unity which characterized, in the beginning, the actual atoms after their radiation throughout the Universal sphere. As these original atoms rushed towards each other in generally straight lines, so let us conceive as at least generally rectilinear, the paths of the system-atoms towards their respective centres of aggregation:—and in this direct drawing together of the systems into clusters, with a similar and simultaneous drawing together of the clusters themselves while undergoing consolidation, we have at length attained the great *Now*—the awful Present—the Existing Condition of the Universe.

Of the still more awful Future a not irrational analogy may guide us in framing an hypothesis. The equilibrium between the centripetal and centrifugal forces of each system, being necessarily destroyed on attainment of a certain proximity to the nucleus of the cluster to which it belongs, there must occur, at once, a chaotic or seemingly chaotic precipitation, of the moons upon the planets, of the planets upon the suns, and of the suns upon the nuclei; and the general result of this precipitation must be the gathering of the myriad now-existing stars of the firmament into an almost infinitely less number of almost infinitely superior spheres. In being immeasurably fewer, the worlds of that day will be immeasurably greater than our own. Then, indeed, amid unfathomable abysses, will be glaring unimaginable suns. But all this will be merely a climactic magnificence foreboding the great End. Of this End the new genesis described can be but a very partial postponement. While undergoing consolidation, the clusters themselves, with a speed prodigiously accumulative, have been rushing towards their own general centre—and now, with a million-fold electric velocity, commensurate only with their material grandeur and with their spiritual passion for oneness, the majestic remnants of the tribe of Stars flash, at length, into a common embrace. The inevitable catastrophe is at hand.

But this catastrophe—what is it? We have seen accomplished the ingathering of the orbs. Henceforward, are we not to understand *one material globe of globes* as comprehending and constituting the Universe? Such a fancy would be altogether at war with every assumption and consideration of this Discourse.

I have already alluded to that absolute *reciprocity of adaptation* which is the idiosyncrasy of the Divine Art—stamping it divine. Up to this point of our reflections, we have been regarding the electrical influence as a something by dint of whose repulsion alone Matter is enabled to exist in that state of diffusion demanded for the fulfilment of its purposes:—so far, in a word, we have been considering the influence in question as ordained for Matter's sake—to subserve the objects of matter. With a perfectly legitimate reciprocity, we are now permitted to look at Matter, as created *solely for the sake of this influence*—solely to serve the objects of this spiritual Ether. Through the aid—by the means—through the agency of Matter, and by dint of its heterogeneity—is this Ether manifested—is *Spirit individualized*. It is merely in the development of this Ether, through heterogeneity, that particular masses of Matter become animate—sensitive—and in the ratio of their heterogeneity;—some reaching a degree of sensitiveness involving what we call *Thought* and thus attaining obviously Conscious Intelligence.

In this view, we are enabled to perceive Matter as a Means—not as an End. Its purposes are thus seen to have been comprehended in its diffusion; and with the return into Unity these purposes cease. The absolutely consolidated globe of globes would be *objectless*:—therefore not for a moment could it continue to exist. Matter, created for an end, would unquestionably, on fulfilment of that end, be Matter no longer. Let us endeavor to understand that it would disappear, and that God would remain all in all.

That every work of Divine conception must cöexist and cöexpire with its particular design, seems to me especially obvious; and I make no doubt that, on perceiving the final globe of globes to be *objectless*, the majority of my readers will be satisfied with my *"therefore* it cannot continue to exist." Nevertheless, as the startling thought of its instantaneous disappearance is one which the most powerful intellect cannot be expected readily to entertain on grounds so decidedly abstract, let us endeavor to look at the idea from some other and more ordinary point of view:—let us see how thoroughly and beautifully it is corroborated in an *à posteriori* consideration of Matter as we actually find it.

I have before said that "Attraction and Repulsion being undeniably the sole properties by which Matter is manifested to Mind, we are justified in assuming that Matter *exists* only as Attraction and Repulsion—in other words that Attraction and Repulsion *are* Matter; there being no conceivable case in which we may not employ the term 'Matter' and the terms 'Attraction' and 'Repulsion' taken together, as equivalent, and therefore convertible, expressions in Logic."

Now the very definition of Attraction implies particularity—the existence of parts, particles, or atoms; for we define it as the tendency of "each atom &c. to every other atom" &c. according to a certain law. Of course where there are *no* parts—where there is absolute Unity—where the tendency to oneness is satisfied—there can be no Attraction:—this has been fully shown, and all Philosophy admits it. When, on fulfilment of its purposes, then, Matter shall have returned into its original condition of *One*—a condition which presupposes the expulsion of the separative Ether, whose province and whose capacity are limited to keeping the atoms apart until that great day when, this Ether being no longer needed, the overwhelming pressure of the finally collective Attraction shall at length just sufficiently predominate and expel it:—when, I say, Matter, finally, expelling the Ether, shall have returned into absolute Unity,—it will then (to speak paradoxically for the moment) be Matter without Attraction and without Repulsion—in other words, Matter without Matter—in other words, again, *Matter no more*. In sinking into Unity, it will sink at once into that Nothingness which, to all finite perception, Unity must be—into that Material Nihility from which alone we can conceive it to have been evoked—to have been *created* by the Volition of God.

I repeat then—Let us endeavor to comprehend that the final globe of globes will instantaneously disappear, and that God will remain all in all.

But are we here to pause? Not so. On the Universal agglomeration and dissolution, we can readily conceive that a new and perhaps totally different series of conditions may ensue—another creation and radiation, returning into itself—another action and rëaction of the Divine Will. Guiding our imaginations by that omniprevalent law of laws, the law of periodicity, are we not, indeed, more than justified in entertaining a belief—let us say, rather, in indulging a hope—that the processes we have here ventured to contemplate will be renewed forever, and forever, and forever; a novel Universe swelling into existence, and then subsiding into nothingness, at every throb of the Heart Divine?

And now—this Heart Divine—what is it? *It is our own.*

Let not the merely seeming irreverence of this idea frighten our souls from that cool exercise of consciousness—from that deep tranquility of self-inspection—through which alone we can hope to attain the presence of this, the most sublime of truths, and look it leisurely in the face.

The *phænomena* on which our conclusions must at this point depend, are merely spiritual shadows, but not the less thoroughly substantial.

We walk about, amid the destinies of our world-existence, encompassed by dim but ever present *Memories* of a Destiny more vast—very distant in the by-gone time, and infinitely awful.

We live out a Youth peculiarly haunted by such shadows; yet never mistaking them for dreams. As Memories we *know* them. *During our Youth* the distinction is too clear to deceive us even for a moment.

So long as this Youth endures, the feeling *that we exist*, is the most natural of all feelings. We understand it *thoroughly*. That there was a period at which we did *not* exist—or, that it might so have happened that we never had existed at all—are the considerations, indeed, which *during this Youth*, we find difficulty in understanding. Why we should *not* exist, is, *up to the epoch of our Manhood*, of all queries the most unanswerable. Existence—self-existence—existence from all Time and to all Eternity—seems, up to the epoch of Manhood, a normal and unquestionable condition:—*seems, because it is.*

But now comes the period at which a conventional World-Reason awakens us from the truth of our dream. Doubt, Surprise and Incomprehensibility arrive at the same moment. They say:—"You live and the time was when you lived not. You have been created. An Intelligence exists greater than your own; and it is only through this Intelligence you live at all." These things we struggle to comprehend and cannot:—*cannot*, because these things, being untrue, are thus, of necessity, incomprehensible.

No thinking being lives who, at some luminous point of his life of thought, has not felt himself lost amid the surges of futile efforts at understanding, or believing, that anything exists *greater than his own soul*. The utter impossibility of any one's soul feeling itself inferior to another; the intense, overwhelming dissatisfaction and rebellion at the thought;—these, with the omniprevalent aspirations at perfection, are but the spiritual, coincident with the material, struggles towards the original Unity—are, to my mind at least, a species of proof far surpassing what Man terms demonstration, that no one soul *is* inferior to another—that nothing is, or can be, superior to any one soul—that each soul is, in part, its own God—its own Creator:—in a word, that God—the material *and* spiritual God—*now* exists solely in the diffused Matter and Spirit of the Universe; and that the regathering of this diffused Matter and Spirit will be but the re-constitution of the *purely Spiritual* and Individual God.

In this view, and in this view alone, we comprehend

the riddles of Divine Injustice—of Inexorable Fate. In this view alone the existence of Evil becomes intelligible; but in this view it becomes more—it becomes endurable. Our souls no longer rebel at a *Sorrow* which we ourselves have imposed upon ourselves, in furtherance of our own purposes—with a view—if even with a futile view—to the extension of our own *Joy*.

I have spoken of *Memories* that haunt us during our Youth. They sometimes pursue us even into our Manhood:—assume gradually less and less indefinite shapes:— now and then speak to us with low voices, saying:

"There was an epoch in the Night of Time, when a still-existent Being existed—one of an absolutely infinite number of similar Beings that people the absolutely infinite domains of the absolutely infinite space. It was not and is not in the power of this Being—any more than it is in your own—to extend, by actual increase, the joy of his Existence; but just as it *is* in your power to expand or to concentrate your pleasures (the absolute amount of happiness remaining always the same) so did and does a similar capability appertain to this Divine Being, who thus passes his Eternity in perpetual variation of Concentrated Self and almost Infinite Self-Diffusion. What you call The Universe of Stars is but his present expansive existence. He now feels his life through an infinity of imperfect pleasures—the partial and pain-intertangled pleasures of those inconceivably numerous things which you designate as his creatures, but which are really but infinite individualizations of Himself. All these creatures—*all*—those whom you term animate, as well as those to which you deny life for no better reason than that you do not behold it in operation—*all* these creatures have, in a greater or less degree, a capacity for pleasure and for pain:—*but the general sum of their sensations is precisely that amount of*

Happiness which appertains by right to the Divine Being when concentrated within Himself. These creatures are all, too, more or less, and more or less obviously, conscious Intelligences; conscious, first, of a proper identity; conscious, secondly and by faint indeterminate glimpses, of an identity with the Divine Being of whom we speak—of an identity with God. Of the two classes of consciousness, fancy that the former will grow weaker, the latter stronger, during the long succession of ages which must elapse before these myriads of individual Intelligences become blended—when the bright stars become blended—into One. Think that the sense of individual identity will be gradually merged in the general consciousness—that Man, for example, ceasing imperceptibly to feel himself Man, will at length attain that awfully triumphant epoch when he shall recognize his existence as that of Jehovah. In the meantime bear in mind that all is Life—Life—Life within Life—the less within the greater, and all within the *Spirit Divine.*"*

* Note—The pain of the consideration that we shall lose our individual identity, ceases at once when we further reflect that the process, as above described, is, neither more nor less than that of the absorption, by each individual intelligence, of all other intelligences (that is, of the Universe) into its own. That God may be all in all, *each* must become God.

Oinos.—Pardon, Agathos, the weakness of a spirit new-fledged with immortality!

Agathos.—You have spoken nothing, my Oinos, for which pardon is to be demanded. Not even here is knowledge a thing of intuition. For wisdom ask of the angels freely, that it may be given!

Oinos.—But in this existence, I dreamed that I should be at once cognizant of all things, and thus at once happy in being cognizant of all.

Agathos.—Ah, not in knowledge is happiness, but in the acquisition of knowledge! In for ever knowing, we are for ever blessed; but to know all were the curse of a fiend.

Oinos.—But does not The Most High know all?

Agathos.—*That* (since he is The Most Happy) must be still the *one* thing unknown even to HIM.

Oinos.—But, since we grow hourly in knowledge, must not *at last* all things be known?

Agathos.—Look down into the abysmal distances!—attempt to force the gaze down the multitudinous vistas of the stars, as we sweep slowly through them thus—and thus—and thus! Even the spiritual vision, is it not at all points arrested by the continuous golden walls of the universe?—the walls of the myriads of the shining bodies that mere number has appeared to blend into unity?

Oinos.—I clearly perceive that the infinity of matter is no dream.

Agathos.—There are *no* dreams in Aidenn—but it is here whispered that, of this infinity of matter, the *sole* purpose is to afford infinite springs, at which the soul may allay the thirst *to know* which is for ever unquenchable within it—since to quench it would be to extinguish the soul's self. Question me then, my Oinos, freely and without fear. Come! we will leave to the left the loud harmony of the Pleiades, and swoop outward from the throne into the starry meadows beyond Orion, where, for pansies and violets, and heart's-ease, are the beds of the triplicate and triple-tinted suns.

Oinos.—And now, Agathos, as we proceed, instruct me! speak to me in the earth's familiar tones! I understood not what you hinted to me, just now, of the modes or of the methods of what, during mortality, we were accustomed to call Creation. Do you mean to say that the Creator is not God?

Agathos.—I mean to say that the Deity does not create.

Oinos.—Explain!

Agathos.—In the beginning *only*, he created. The seeming creatures which are now, throughout the universe, so perpetually springing into being, can only be considered as the mediate or indirect, not as the direct or immediate results of the Divine creative power.

Oinos.—Among men, my Agathos, this idea would be considered heretical in the extreme.

Agathos.—Among angels, my Oinos, it is seen to be simply true.

Oinos.—I can comprehend you thus far—that certain operations of what we term Nature, or the natural laws, will, under certain conditions, give rise to that which has all the *appearance* of creation. Shortly before the final over-throw of the earth, there were, I well remember, many very successful experiments in what some philosophers were weak enough to denominate the creation of animalculæ.

Agathos.—The cases of which you speak were, in fact, instances of the secondary creation—and of the *only* species of creation which has ever been, since the first word spoke into existence the first law.

Oinos.—Are not the starry worlds that, from the abyss of nonentity, burst hourly forth into the heavens—are not these stars, Agathos, the immediate handiwork of the King?

Agathos.—Let me endeavor, my Oinos, to lead you, step by step, to the conception I intend. You are well aware that, as no thought can perish, so no act is without infinite result. We moved our hands, for example, when we were dwellers on the earth, and, in so doing, we gave vibration to the atmosphere which engirdled it. This vibration was indefinitely extended, till it gave impulse to every particle of the earth's air, which thenceforward, *and for ever*, was actuated by the one movement of the hand. This fact the mathematicians of our globe well knew. They made the special effects, indeed, wrought in the fluid by special impulses, the subject of exact calculation—so that it became easy to determine in what precise period an impulse of given extent would engirdle the orb, and impress (for ever) every atom of the atmosphere circumambient. Retrograding, they found no difficulty, from a given effect, under given conditions, in determining the value of the original impulse. Now the mathematicians who saw that the results of any given impulse were absolutely endless—and who saw that a portion of these results were accurately traceable through the agency of algebraic analysis—who saw, too, the facility of the retrogradation—these men saw, at the same time, that this species of analysis itself, had within itself a capacity for indefinite progress—that there were no bounds conceivable to its advancement and applicability, except within the intellect of him who advanced or applied it. But at this point our mathematicians paused.

Oinos.—And why, Agathos, should they have proceeded?

Agathos.—Because there were some considerations of deep interest, beyond. It was deducible from what they knew, that to a being of infinite understanding—one to whom the *perfection* of the algebraic analysis lay unfolded—there could be no difficulty in tracing every impulse given the air—and the ether through the air—to the remotest consequences at any even infinitely remote epoch of time. It is indeed demonstrable that every such impulse *given the air*, must, *in the end*, impress every individual thing that exists *within the universe*;—and the being of infinite understanding—the being whom we have imagined—might trace the remote undulations of the impulse—trace them upward and onward in their influences upon all particles of all matter—upward and onward for ever in their modifications of old forms—or in other words, *in their creation of new*—until he found them reflected—unimpressive *at last*—back from the throne of the Godhead. And not only could such a being do this, but at any epoch, should a given result be afforded him—should one of these numberless comets, for example, be presented to his inspection,—he could have no difficulty in determining, by the analytic retrogradation, to what original impulse it was due. This power of retrogradation in its absolute fulness and perfection—this faculty of referring at *all* epochs, *all* effects to *all* causes—is of course the prerogative of the Deity alone—but in every variety of degree, short of the absolute perfection, is the power itself exercised by the whole host of the Angelic Intelligences.

Oinos.—But you speak merely of impulses upon the air.

Agathos.—In speaking of the air, I referred only to the earth:—but the general proposition has reference to impulses upon the ether—which, since it pervades, and alone pervades all space, is thus the great medium of *creation*.

Oinos.—Then all motion, of whatever nature, creates.

Agathos.—It must: but a true philosophy has long taught that the source of all motion is thought—and the source of all thought is—

Oinos.—God.

Agathos.—I have spoken to you, Oinos, as to a child of the fair Earth which lately perished—of impulses upon the atmosphere of the Earth.

Oinos.—You did.

Agathos.—And while I thus spoke, did there not cross your mind some thought of the *physical power of words*? Is not every word an impulse on the air?

Oinos.—But why, Agathos, do you weep?—and why— oh why do your wings droop as we hover above this fair star—which is the greenest and yet most terrible of all we have encountered in our flight? Its brilliant flowers look like a fairy dream—but its fierce volcanoes like the passions of a turbulent heart.

Agathos.—They *are!*—they *are!* This wild star—it is now three centuries since with clasped hands, and with streaming eyes, at the feet of my beloved—I spoke it— with a few passionate sentences—into birth. Its brilliant flowers *are* the dearest of all unfulfilled dreams, and its raging volcanoes *are* the passions of the most turbulent and unhallowed of hearts.

BIOGRAPHICAL NOTE

NOTE ON THE TEXTS

NOTES

INDEX OF TITLES &
FIRST LINES

Edgar Allan Poe was born in Boston, Massachusetts, on January 19, 1809. He was the second of three children of Elizabeth Arnold and David Poe, who were traveling actors. Poe's father abandoned the family in 1809, and his mother moved frequently before her death in Richmond, Virginia, in 1811. Poe was separated from his siblings and taken into the home of the Richmond tobacco merchant John Allan and his wife, Frances; the Allans served as foster parents but did not legally adopt him. Accompanying the Allans to Great Britain, Poe attended schools in London from 1815 to 1820 before returning with the family to Richmond in 1820. Poe entered the University of Virginia in 1826; he lost money while gambling, and Allan refused to honor the debt. Poe moved to Boston, where he anonymously published his first book of verse, *Tamerlane and Other Poems* (1827). He enlisted in the U.S. Army under the assumed name Edgar A. Perry, and was stationed at Fort Moultrie, South Carolina. At the request of his dying foster mother he was partially reconciled with Allan, who helped him secure an appointment to the U.S. Military Academy at West Point. While waiting for news of his appointment, he lived in Baltimore with his brother and his aunt Maria Clemm. His second volume of poetry, *Al Aaraaf, Tamerlane and Minor Poems*, appeared in 1829. He was dismissed from West Point after eight months for neglect of duty. *Poems by Edgar A. Poe: Second Edition* (1831) was published in New York. Returning to Baltimore, he lived with Mrs. Clemm and her eight-year-old daughter, Virginia. He began to publish short fiction in magazines, and achieved recognition in 1833 when "MS. Found in a Bottle" won a competition; he obtained an editorial position with the *Southern Literary Messenger* in 1835 and contributed stories, book reviews, and poems. In September 1835 he married Virginia, then 13. Disputes with the publisher led to Poe's resignation from the *Messenger*, and he moved to New York with Virginia and Mrs. Clemm in 1837. A year later he moved to Philadelphia, where he became co-editor of *Burton's Gentleman's Magazine*, contributing such stories as "The Fall of the House of Usher" and "William Wilson." A first collection of stories, *Tales of the Grotesque and Arabesque*, appeared in 1839. After leaving *Burton's* he became literary editor of *Graham's Magazine* (1841–42). Poe won a prize in 1843 for "The Gold-Bug," and the following year he moved back to New York where he worked for the *New-York Evening Mirror* and, as editor, *The Broadway Journal*. He achieved fame as a poet with the publication of "The Raven" in the *Mirror* in 1845, followed by the collection *The Raven and Other Poems*. His public accusations of plagiarism against Henry Wadsworth Longfellow involved him in protracted controversy. After years of illness, Virginia died of tuberculosis in 1847. The next year Poe published the metaphysical treatise *Eureka*, and returned to Richmond. In October 1849 Poe stopped in Baltimore on the way to New York on literary business; he was found in a delirious condition and died four days later on October 7.

NOTE ON THE TEXTS

The poems presented in this volume are arranged in approxi-
mate order of compostion. Because Poe often revised his writ-
ings, this volume prints versions of works containing his latest
revisions. The source of the text of each title is identified be-
low. The dates in parentheses indicate the year of first publica-
tion or, where known, composition. The names of frequently
recurring sources are keyed to the following abbreviations:

Mabbott   *Collected Works of Edgar Allan Poe*, 3 vols., ed. Thomas Ollive
           Mabbott (Cambridge, Mass.: Harvard University Press, 1969
           & 1978)

ROP   *The Raven and Other Poems* (New York: Wiley and Putnam,
           1845)

Stovall   *The Poems of Edgar Allan Poe*, ed. Floyd Stovall (Charlottesville,
           Va.: University Press of Virginia, 1965)

TOP   *Tamerlane and Other Poems* (Boston: Calvin F. S. Thomas—
           Printer, 1827)

Works   *The Works of the Late Edgar Allan Poe*, 4 vols., ed. Rufus Wilmot
           Griswold (New York: J. S. Redfield, 1850–56)

POETRY

Tamerlane (1827)	ROP
Song (1827)	ROP
Dreams (1827)	Mabbott, I, 68–69; from 1828 MS
Spirits of the Dead (1827)	*Burton's Gentleman's Magazine* (Philadelphia), July 1839
Evening Star (1827)	TOP
"Stanzas" (1827)	TOP
A Dream (1827)	TOP
"The Happiest Day" (1827)	TOP
The Lake—To —— (1827)	ROP
Sonnet—To Science (1829)	ROP
Al Aaraaf (1829)	ROP
Romance (1829)	ROP
To —— ("The bowers whereat") (1829)	ROP
To the River —— (1828)	ROP
To —— ("I heed not") (1829)	Mabbott, I, 137; from 1828–49 MS
Fairy-Land (1829)	ROP
"Alone" (c. 1829)	Mabbott, I, 146-47; from 1829 MS
"To Isaac Lea" (1829)	Arthur H. Quinn, *Edgar Allan Poe: A Critical Biography* (New York: D. Appleton Century, 1941), 138–43; from 1829 MS letter
Elizabeth (c. 1829)	*Complete Poems of Edgar Allan Poe*, ed. James H. Whitty (Boston: Houghton Mifflin, 1911), 140
An Acrostic (c. 1829)	Whitty, 141; from c. 1829 MS
To Helen (1831)	ROP
Israfel (1831)	Mabbott, I, 175–77; from ROP-Lorimer Graham copy, 1849
The Sleeper (1831)	Stovall, 52; from ROP-Lorimer Graham
The Valley of Unrest (1831)	ROP
The City in the Sea (1831)	ROP
Lenore (1831)	*Richmond Daily Whig*, Sept. 18, 1849
To One in Paradise (c. 1833)	Stovall, 59; from ROP-Lorimer Graham
Hymn (c. 1833)	*Works*; identical to ROP-Lorimer Graham
Enigma (1833)	*Baltimore Saturday Visiter*, Feb. 2, 1833

PROSE

Preface (Tamerlane and Other Poems)	TOP
Letter to Mr. —— ——	*Poems* (1831)
Preface (The Raven and Other Poems)	ROP
from The Poetic Principle	*Sartain's Union Magazine*, Oct. 1850
from Review of *Orion*, by R. H. Horne	*Graham's Magazine* (Philadelphia), March
from Review of *Alciphron*, by Thomas Moore	*Burton's Gentleman's Magazine*, Jan. 1840
from Chapter of Suggestions	*The Opal* (New York, 1845)
from Marginalia	*Democratic Review*, December 1844; *Graham's Magazine*, March 1846; *Southern Literary Messenger*, May 1849
from Eureka: A Prose Poem (1848)	Roland W. Nelson, "The Definitive Edition of Edgar Allan Poe's *Eureka: A Prose Poem*" (Ph.D. dissertation, Bowling Green State University, 1974)
The Power of Words (1845)	*Broadway Journal* (New York), Oct. 25, 1845

The following is a list of pages where a stanza break coincides with the foot of the page (except where such breaks are apparent from the regular stanzaic structure of the poem): 3, 4, 6, 12, 36, 58, 60.

Typographical errors in the source texts corrected: 16.12, light-such; 55.27, streams; 58.25, wanlight; 83.3, Half; 89.13, way.

NOTES

20.9   Sonnet—To Science]   Poe included a footnote to the poem: "Private reasons—some of which have reference to the sin of plagiarism, and others to the date of Tennyson's first poems—have induced me, after some hesitation, to re-publish these, the crude compositions of my earliest boyhood. They are printed *verbatim*—without alteration from the original edition—the date of which is too remote to be judiciously acknowledged.—E.A.P."

44.1   "To Isaac Lea"]   Written in a letter to the publisher Isaac Lea (May 27, 1829), of the Philadelphia firm of Carey and Lea, whom Poe sought unsuccessfully to interest in bringing out his second volume of poems.

44.6–45.1   Elizabeth . . . An Acrostic]   Both of these poems were written in the album of Poe's cousin Elizabeth Rebecca Herring. The initials "L. E. L." in line 3 of "An Acrostic" are those of the then-popular poet Letitia E. Landon.

54.5   Peccavimus]   We have sinned (Psalm 106:6).

56.14   Enigma]   The first letters of the answers to each of the puzzles spell "Shakspeare."

59.23   To F——s S. O——d]   Frances Sargent Osgood (1811–50), wife of the well-known portrait painter Samuel Stillman Osgood, who painted Poe's portrait, was famous in her own right as a prolific poet. "To

F——" and "A Valentine to —— —— ——" were also written for Mrs. Osgood.

62.2   Fair isle]   Zakinthos, in the Ionian group.

62.15   "Isola d'oro! Fior di Levante!"]   "Golden isle! Flower of the Levant!" The phrases were used by Chateaubriand to describe the island in his *Itinéraire de Paris à Jérusalem* (1811).

63.12   Porphyrogene]   According to the *New English Dictionary*, the unique occurrence of the word. Apparently Poe was acquainted with the etymology of its basic meaning of "regal": in the imperial palace of Constantinople childbirth took place in a special room with purple drapes, the *Porphyra*. Royal children were thus literally "born in the purple."

75.1   balm in Gilead]   Jeremiah 8:22; see also Genesis 37:25.

77.17   To M. L. S——]   Mary Louise Shew, the nurse who attended Virginia Poe during her last illness and later Poe himself.

78.9   To —— —— ——]   Written for and about Mary Louise Shew. The poem contains three literary allusions: "the power of words" refers to Poe's prose fantasy of that title; "dew that hangs like pearls on Hermon hill" is from George Peele's play *David and Bethsabe* (1599); "the sweetest voice of all God's creatures" refers to the epigraph of Poe's "Israfel."

83.1   An Enigma]   One of Poe's benefactors following Virginia's death in 1847 was Sarah Anna Lewis, the 14 letters of whose name are methodically staggered down the successive lines of this sonnet.

83.11   tuckermanities]   The reference is to Boston-born author Henry T. Tuckerman (1813–71), known for his sonnets.

87.20   Helen]   Sarah Helen Powers, whom Poe saw in the garden of her house in Providence, Rhode Island, in 1845 but did not meet until the fall of 1848.

91.1   Annie]   Nancy B. Richmond of Lowell, Massachusetts.

96.1   My Mother]   Maria Poe Clemm, mother of Virgina, who was Poe's aunt and mother-in-law.

96.16   Annabel Lee]   The text is that of the last manuscript, dated September 26, 1849, which differs in one way from earlier versions in its revision of the final line originally used: "In her tomb by the sounding sea."

98.1   Scenes from "Politian"]   Poe's only verse drama remains unfinished. Of the 11 scenes he wrote, he chose to publish only the five scenes included here. The plot of "Politian" follows a series of events that took place in Frankfort, Kentucky, in 1825. "The Kentucky Tragedy," as it came to be called, attracted much popular interest at the time.

121.24–25   Nos . . . nihil]   We know those things to be nothing.

126.21–22   de . . . aliis]   Concerning everything that can be written about, and other things as well.

127.29   Tantæne animis?]   An abbreviated allusion to Virgil's line, "In heavenly breasts do such fierce passions dwell." (*Aeneid*, I, 11)

129.10–11   wagon . . . turkeys.]   The sentence alludes to Wordsworth's poem "The Waggoner"; Sophocles' being called a bee (poetry as honey completing the metaphor); the Oedipus plays (the name Oedipus meaning "swollen foot"); the notion that in the Sophoclean fragment *Meleager* guinea fowl make up the chorus.

129.14–16   "J'ai trouve . . . nient,"]   "I have often found that most sects are correct in much of what they uphold, but not in what they deny."

129.26   Corcyra]   Corfu.

133.18–19   Pure . . . Sense.]   The tripartite paradigm of Immanuel Kant in his introduction to *The Critique of Judgment* (1793).

134.27   Abbaté Gravina]   Gian Vincenzo Gravina (1664–1718), Italian writer and jurist, noted for his theory of poetics (*Ragion poetica*, 1708).

138.23   Fourier's dreams]   Charles Fourier (1772–1837), French social theorist. Brook Farm, in Roxbury, Massachusetts, was one of the utopian settlements based on his principles.

INDEX OF TITLES
AND FIRST LINES